WHY DO DOGS HAVE WET NOSES?

WHY DO DOGS HAVE WET NOSES?
and Other Imponderables™ of Everyday Life

David Feldman

Illustrated by Kassie Schwan

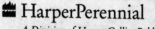
HarperPerennial
A Division of HarperCollinsPublishers

First HarperPerennial edition published 1991.

Designed by Cassandra J. Pappas

The Library of Congress has catalogued the hardcover edition as follows:

Feldman, David, 1950–
    Why do dogs have wet noses? and other imponderables of everyday life / David Feldman : illustrated by Kassie Schwan.—1st ed.
        p.   cm.
    Includes index.
    ISBN 0-06-016293-7
    1. Questions and answers.   I. Title.
AG195.F47   1990
031.02—dc20   89-46529

ISBN 0-06-092111-0 (pbk.)

    92 93 94 95   MB   10 9 8 7 6 5

For Jim Trupin

Contents

CONTENTS

CONTENTS

CONTENTS

CONTENTS   **xv**

Preface

We live in an age of lasers and quarks. We are supposedly over-loaded with information. But there is much we don't know. Like why does a green bar of soap yield white suds? Or why have most airlines stopped serving honey roasted peanuts?

As long as there are humans, there will be Imponderables, little mysteries of everyday life that drive you nuts—until you get the answers. Our mission is to stamp out Imponderability; this isn't an easy task, but luckily our readers have made it a collaborative enterprise.

Virtually all of the mysteries in this book were sent in by readers of the first three volumes of *Imponderables*. In the Frust-ables section, readers offer their help in answering ten frustrating Imponderables that we haven't been able to solve.

And for those of you who want to let us have it, the letters section is the place.

How do we entice potential coconspirators? If you are the first person to submit an Imponderable that we use in the next book, or are the first to solve a Frustable, you'll receive a free, autographed copy of the book, along with an acknowledgment.

The last page of the book tells you how to get in touch with us. But for now, fasten your emotional seat belt and enjoy. *Imponderables* can be a fun and bumpy ride.

Imponderables

What Are Gnats Doing When They Swarm?

Gnats are not the only living things that swarm. Birds do it. And bees do it. So it shouldn't be too surprising to learn that those gnats aren't freaking out or doing an insect variation of slam dancing when they swarm. Those are male gnats looking for female companionship.

Like the boys in *Saturday Night Fever*, flashing their gold chains and hairy chests, male gnats figure that no hot-blooded female anthropod could possibly resist their charms when they strut their stuff together. Amazingly, it works. At least, we can say with authority that there is no shortage of gnats.

One question persists, though. If the purpose of the swarming display is to find a female, why do all the males compete with each other in a swarm when the female of the species is probably telling her best friend, "When they're swarming, all boy-gnats look alike."

Maybe swarming isn't the most efficient means for male

gnats to find a mate, but then pack cruising in bars isn't the most efficient method either. Maybe male gnats, like their human counterparts, need friends along to steel their courage.

Submitted by Charles, a caller on the Larry Mantle show, KPPC-FM, Pasadena, California.

Why Do Manufacturers Place Underwear Labels Inside the Center of the Back Where They Rub Uncomfortably on a Person's Spine?

When we posed this imponderable to our illustrious illustrator, Kassie Schwan, she quickly answered, "So that you know which way to put your underwear on." Yes, Kas, but this begs the question. Which sadist decided that the label had to be put in a place designed to rub against our delicate backsides?

As usual with such matters, economics rears its ugly head. Underwear is a low profit margin item; manufacturers are eager to cut costs in any way possible. It is cheaper to print the size on a label attached to the garment than it would be to print the size on each polymer bag. This way, the label doubles as the size indicator at the retail store.

At least one person was willing to state that he was unashamed of the industry practice. George Weldon, of underwear giant Munsingwear, said that his company's labels are made of 100% cotton, and are so soft that consumers can't tell whether the label is on the outside or inside.

You know something? He's right. In the interest of science, we tested his thesis and found that we could not tell whether the label was on the outside, inside, or, in one case, torn off completely.

A caller on a talk show once pleaded: "Why can't manufacturers put the labels on the outside of the back?" Weldon says that Munsingwear considered it, but consumers fear exposing their size inadvertently to the scrutiny and amusement of the public.

Submitted by Kay Nelson of Huntington Beach, California.

When a Letter Is Sent from the United States to Greece, Does Greece Receive any Money from the U.S. for Delivering It?

Much to our surprise, yes.

Ernest J. Collins, of the USPS's Office of Classification and Rates Administration, explains what is called the "terminal dues system":

> Foreign countries receive reimbursement for mail they process and deliver which is in excess of the mail which they send to the United States. For example, if during a given period Greece sent to the United States 10,000 kilograms of mail and the United States sent 12,000 kilograms to Greece, there would be an imbalance of 2,000 kilograms. The United States would reimburse Greece for the extra 2,000 kilograms. The reimbursement rate is currently $3.28 per kilogram.

The system does not differentiate between the two types of international mail, "LC" (letters and cards) and "AO" (publications). The terminal dues system reduces to a formula of about a nickel for delivering one half-ounce letter and about 30 times that much for delivering a one-pound magazine. A USPS press release complains that

> this type of terminal dues structure does not represent the real costs of delivering these different kinds of mails, since half-ounce letters cannot be handled and delivered for a nickel and it does not cost $1.57 to deliver a single magazine.

This imbalance of payments has caused political problems in the international postal community. Industrial nations, such as the

United States, lobby for greater compensation for letters, while small countries want to preserve the status quo.

The reason for the disagreement, of course, is purely financial. The U.S. has a large net outflow of publications and a huge net inflow of letters and postcards. The U.S. must subsidize the delivery of its international letters while simultaneously paying much more to foreign countries to deliver American publications than it really costs them to process and deliver.

The United States Postal Service isn't the only government arm that loses money because of this terminal dues system. The IRS wants its share too. Many American publishers have found it cheaper to relocate their printing facilities in foreign countries than pay punitive international postage fees. Other publishers freight items to the foreign country and then pay that country's local postage rates.

Because the international organization that arbitrates these matters has a one-country/one-vote policy (like the General Assembly of the United Nations), the little countries were able to block efforts to increase compensation for delivering letters.

But a Solomon-like solution has been agreed upon and will go into effect on January 1, 1991. The current flat rate will be continued until a "threshold amount" of 150 metric tons of annual mail is sent out of a country (third world countries do not send out this much). After 150 metric tons, the compensation will better reflect the actual cost of processing and delivering that type of mail.

Submitted by Bob Hatch of Seattle, Washington. Thanks also to Sharon Roberts of Ames, Quebec.

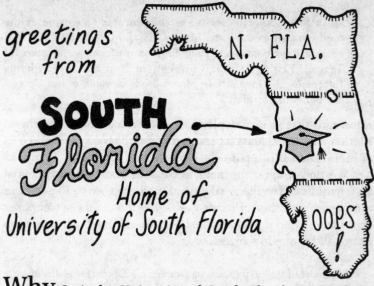

greetings from

SOUTH *Florida*

Home of University of South Florida

N. FLA.

OOPS!

Why Isn't the University of South Florida in Southern Florida?

Yes, folks. The University of South Florida is located in Tampa, smack dab in the middle (north-southwise, at least) of Florida. Maybe our simple peasant heritage is betraying us, but we too wondered why an institution of higher learning couldn't get its geographical location right.

We received a witty letter from Robert L. Allen, director of USF office of public affairs, in which he demonstrates that there was a modicum of logic in the name choice:

> When the University of South Florida was founded in 1956, there were already three other state-supported universities in Florida. They were Florida A&M University (Tallahassee) and Florida State University (Tallahassee), both in northwestern Florida, and the University of Florida (Gainesville) in north central Florida.
>
> At the time, the University of South Florida was the southernmost university in the Florida State University system. The pow-

ers that be did not foresee the establishment of universities in the southern part of the state. Since 1956, the University of Central Florida has been established in Orlando [not too far north of Tampa], Florida Atlantic University in Boca Raton and Florida International University in Miami [both far south of the University of South Florida].

Allen adds that "we generally describe our location as southwest Florida," which at least indicates that Tampa is on the west coast of Florida and still retains the USF initials.

We find it amazing that the trustees of the Florida school system didn't have the wisdom and marketing savvy to put more campuses in southern Florida long ago. After all, these campuses could have offered package deals of tuition plus Easter vacation frolics all for one low price.

Submitted by Jerry Kiewe of Lauderdale Lakes (far south of Tampa, by the way), Florida.

Why Are Racquetballs Blue?

Larry Josefowicz, of Wilson Sporting Goods Co., told *Imponderables* that the dark blue color is the most easily discernible. Light colors fade into the wooden floors and white or cream walls of a racquetball court. Considering how fast a racquetball moves during a game, the choice of colors becomes a safety, as well as a playability, issue.

Wilson and its competitors tested other colors, but none combined visibility with customer preference like the present color. Brad Patterson, executive director of the Racquetball Manufacturers Association, adds that at one time, black and dark green racquetballs were tested, but they marked the walls. Patterson doesn't see any other color stealing blue's thunder in the near future:

The other reason it will be difficult to ever phase in any other color ball is simply player preference. It is akin to yellow tennis balls now [yellow tennis balls were also introduced to improve visibility, especially for indoor and nighttime tennis]. The players simply prefer blue, since that is the color they grew up with . . .

Submitted by Gary Fradkin of Carmel, New York.

Is There Any Rhyme or Reason to the Numbers Assigned to Federal Tax Forms? For Example, How Did the Most Prominent Form Get the Number 1040?

We heard from no less of a source than the chief of the Publishing Services Branch of the Internal Revenue Service, Hugh W. Kent, Jr. He prefaced his explanation by writing:

> We wish we could reciprocate with a Gothic tale of mystique, cloaked in a night fog like the one that hovered in the woods outside Dr. Frankenstein's castle.

Now we know the IRS has been accused of sadistic tendencies in the past, so as conscientious and heretofore unaudited taxpayers, we just want you, the reader, to realize that Mr. Kent is merely joking. He doesn't really wish to scare the hardworking taxpayers of America with ominous tales of nefarious IRS plots. On the contrary, he is demonstrating the fact that IRS officials have wonderful senses of humor. We're sure that Mr. Kent and the other fine people at the IRS understand that we were conducting legitimate business during that weeklong trip to Disney World last year. Researching Imponderables, you know.

Kirk Markland, also with the Publishing Services Branch, told us that the IRS decided on a four-digit numbering system for their forms. The rest, as Mr. Kent continues, is history:

> For stock, revision, and other control purposes, we number our forms in numerical sequence. Thus, when the first tax law

AND OTHER IMPONDERABLES

became effective in 1913, we merely numbered the new individual income tax form with the next number in sequence, which happened to be 1040. To preclude having large gaps in the sequential order of form numbers, our forms' numbering system allows us to reuse numbers as old forms become obsolete.

Neil Patton, chief of the Taxpayer Information and Education Branch of the IRS, sent us a copy of the first Form 1040, which was considerably simpler than today's "short form." One page asked taxpayers to itemize the types of income they accrued in 1913; another page asked about deductions in only seven categories. And the front page did not task the mathematical skills of the taxpayer: It asked him or her to subtract deductions from gross income, account for withheld taxes, and calculate the tax on a scale that will evoke nostalgia for all. The highest tax rate, for those earning more than $500,000 in net income, was all of six percent.

Submitted by Boyd Briskin of Riverside, California. Thanks also to Michael Gempe of Elmhurst, Illinois.

Why Does Wood "Pop" When Put on a Fire?

John A. Pitcher, director of the Hardwood Research Council, was kind enough to tackle this burning Imponderable:

Wood pops when put on a fire because there are little pockets of sap, pitch [resin], or other volatiles that are contained in the wood. As the wood surface is heated and burns, heat is transferred to the sap or pitch deeper in the wood.

The sap or pitch first liquefies, then vaporizes as the temperature increases. Gasses expand rapidly when heated and put tremendous pressure on the walls of the pitch pocket. When the pressure gets high enough, the pocket walls burst and the characteristic sound is heard.

Submitted by Patric Conroy of Walnut Creek, California.

WHY DO DOGS HAVE WET NOSES?

Why Does a Fire Create a Crackling Sound? Is There Any Reason Why a Fire Cracks Most When First Lit?

Of course, "pops" are not unrelated to "crackles." John Pitcher explains that the larger the sap or pitch pockets in the wood, the bigger the pop; but if there are smaller but more numerous pockets, the wood will crackle instead.

The reason most fires crackle most when first lit is that the smaller pieces of wood, used as kindling, heat up quickly. The inside sap pockets are penetrated and crackle immediately. Big pieces of wood burn much more slowly, with fewer, intermittent, but louder pops.

For those of you who are, pardon the expression, "would-be" connoisseurs of lumber acoustics, Pitcher provided *Imponderables* readers with a consumer's guide:

> There are distinct differences in the popping characteristics of woods. High on the list of poppers is tamarack or larch. Most conifers are ready poppers. On the other hand, hardwoods, such as ash, elm, and oak, tend to burn quietly, with only an occasionally tastefully subdued pop. You might call them poopers rather than poppers.

Submitted by Andrew F. Garruto of Kinnelon, New Jersey.

Why Did the Chinese First Use Chopsticks?

The conventional wisdom on this subject is that the Chinese consider it the chef's duty to carve meat or slice vegetables into bitesize morsels. Chopsticks were then invented to serve as efficient tools to pick up morsels of food and rice. But there is much evidence to suggest that their use was originally motivated not by aesthetics but by practical considerations.

Chopsticks were introduced sometime during the Chou Dynasty, probably a century or so before the birth of Christ. Until the Chou Dynasty, stir frying did not exist. But China faced a serious fuel (i.e., wood) shortage. Forests were cut down to clear land for agriculture to feed a burgeoning population.

Stir frying developed as the most efficient method to use the least amount of wood as fuel for the shortest period of time. Because the food was cut before stir frying, the meat and vegetables cooked much faster than by other methods.

During the Chou Dynasty, few people owned tables (a luxury, especially with the wood shortage), so a utensil was needed that would allow diners to eat with one hand only—the other

WHY DO DOGS HAVE WET NOSES?

hand was needed to hold the bowl of rice. Because most Chinese dishes have sauces, chopsticks enabled users to scoop up food without getting goop all over their fingers. And now chopsticks allow non-Orientals the opportunity to propel goop all over the tablecloths of Chinese restaurants.

And why did the Chinese decide to use chopsticks in the middle of this supposed wood shortage? Only some of the chopsticks were made of wood. More were made of ivory and bone.

Why Have Most Airlines Stopped Serving Honey Roasted Peanuts and Resumed Giving Away Salted and Dry Roasted Peanuts?

Sara Dornacker, media relations manager of United Airlines, told *Imponderables* that "cocktail snacks are rotated periodically to give frequent fliers some variety." United Airlines served honey roasted peanuts for five consecutive years but withdrew them for about one year while they gave "lightly salted peanuts" a chance. But in February, 1990, United brought back honey roasted peanuts and is hedging their decision now by alternating them with pretzels. Only time will tell whether passengers conditioned to legumes with their drinks will respond to starch.

But another source offers an alternative explanation for why honey roasted peanuts seem to have been withdrawn from most airlines' food service at around the same time. Phillip S. Cooke, executive administrator of Inflight Food Service Association, reports that passengers

> repeatedly commented in survey after survey that they did not like the smell created in the cabin when all of the passengers opened those little bags simultaneously. Apparently, honey roasted peanuts create a rather sickly sweet smell, although I must confess that I have never noticed it and it has certainly never bothered me personally.

It's never bothered us either. We were having a hard enough time trying to open up those blasted little bags with our fingernails and/or teeth.

Submitted by Deborah J. Huth of San Jose, California.

Why Don't Magazines Put Page Numbers on Every Page?

Magazine publishers *would* like to put a number on every page of their magazine. But many publishers freely agree to withhold pagination for full-page advertisements, particularly for "bleed" ads, in which the material covers the entire page. In a standard ad, an outside border usually allows for pagination without interfering with photographs or artwork. But many advertising agencies demand that their image-enhancing bleed ads not be marred by anything as mundane as a page number; publishers contractually accede to this requirement.

High-circulation magazines often publish many different editions. When you encounter letters after a page number (e.g., 35A, 35B, 35C), you are reading a section designed for a particular demographic or geographic group. Readers often find these editions annoying, because they impede the flow of the magazine (try finding page 36 when the regional edition occupies pages 35A through 35Q).

By customizing their editions, magazines can not only attract advertisers who might be uninterested or cannot afford inserting messages in a national edition, but can charge considerably more per thousand readers reached. If *Fortune* printed an edition targeted at accountants, for example, a software company with a new accounting package might be convinced to advertise in this edition but would not find it cost-effective to try the national edition. Even nonbleed full-page ads designed for regional or demographic editions are rarely numbered, since one ad might appear on several different page numbers in different editions.

J. J. Hanson, chairman and CEO of Hanson Publishing Group, Inc., adds that another reason for omitting pagination is that some ads are actually preprinted by the advertiser and inserted in the magazine: "Often those preprinted inserts are prepared before the publisher knows which page number would be appropriate." Scratch and sniff perfume strips and liquor ads with laser effects are two common examples.

At a time when one designer-jeans advertiser might book ten consecutive, nonpaginated pages, and regional, demographic, and advertising supplements can dot a single issue of a magazine, finding a page number can be a mine field for readers. But a gold mine for the publishers.

Submitted by Samuel F. Pugh of Indianapolis, Indiana. Thanks also to Karin Norris of Salinas, California; and Gloria A. Quigley of Chicago, Illinois.

West Side Fish Story

OKAY, GANG! WE AGREE TO A TRUCE!

Why Don't the Small Fish in a Large Aquarium Have the Gills Scared out of Them Every Time a Big Fish, Such as a Shark, Swims By?

Every time we go to a public aquarium, we ask this question of anyone who looks even quasiofficial. We understand that a huge shark might not be a natural predator of a small fish. But then an elephant isn't *our* natural predator. And if an elephant started chasing us down the street, you'd better believe we would duck and cover.

Every one of those quasiofficials at the aquariums reported that the little fish didn't seem the least bit frightened by the sharks. We contacted some fish experts to discuss this phenomenon and in unison they echoed the same sentiments: Little fish don't tend to be any more frightened by sharks than mosquitoes are of humans.

Why not? Life in an aquarium, like the economy, is largely a matter of supply and demand. Little fish are not going to be eaten unless there is demand (i.e., hungry sharks). But aquarium heads, like some overactive presidents, tinker with the supply-demand equation. As an economist might put it, an aquarium is not a free market. The aquarium cuts demand by feeding the sharks, producing an artificial oversupply. R. Bruce Gebhardt, secretary and past president of the North American Native Fishes Association, explains:

> It doesn't behoove the manager of a public aquarium to replace smaller livestock all the time. It's too expensive and time-consuming . . . so the tank manager will feed the sharks. The sharks will come to rely on easy feeding rather than actually working for their food. If they're full, they're less likely to want to feed on other fish and make threatening moves towards them.

As the sharks (or other large predators) become progressively lazier, the small fish become emboldened, seeing themselves no longer as appetizers but rather as smaller but equal roommates in the tank. So the small fish comprise an ample but elusive supply for the sharks.

All of the authorities we contacted agreed that fish seem to have a developed sense or instinct that lets them know when they are in danger. Dr. Robert R. Rofen, of the Aquatic Research Institute, refers to the intelligence of fish ("they are smart enough to analyze whether they are in danger or not"). Gerry Carr, Director of Species Research for the International Game Fish Association, testifies to the adaptability of small fish:

> Little fish naturally do not want to be eaten and will vanish in a blink the moment the big fish begin to give off hunger signals. I don't know exactly how the little fish pick up on this, but they do. Maybe the shark's movements and vibrations change and this is picked up by the lateral line of the smaller fish. Maybe the shark's stomach growls (just kidding, but who knows). Fish have very active perception and can recognize and react to vibrations, temperature changes, and chemical changes in the water, all of which may play a part in alerting the potential sushi [Hey! *We'll* do the jokes here] meals of their impending danger.

One can observe large bass swimming casually in a lake with swarms of small fish that are their natural food, and the small fish will show no fear. But when the dinner bell rings, everything changes.

Carr adds that despite the shark's fearsome image, other fish, such as large groupers, would pose a much greater threat to small fish. Groupers are veritable vacuum cleaners in aquariums and are relatively oblivious to other fishes if they are well fed. Even sharks will backslide if in a frenzy or in the mood for a snack if the small fish make themselves easy prey.

Gerry Carr suggests that fishes, both large and small, "are not truly 'natural enemies' as we understand the term. The big fish just get hungry and eat the little fish. No grudge is involved and no offense is taken." Although it's futile to hold a grudge or take offense when you happen to be being digested in the offender's stomach at the moment.

But don't feel too sorry for the small fish. As Gebhardt points out, small fish

> can easily outmaneuver the shark in a relatively confined space. If they have reef structure to escape to quickly, they may be confident enough in their own invulnerability to swim unalarmed. If the fish are small enough, they wouldn't be worth the shark's effort. There's no point in a shark spending more energy chasing prey than he gets from eating it.

What Is the Purpose of the Orange Balls You Sometimes See on Power Lines?

Next to pairs of tied-up tennis shoes (why *do* kids throw them up there?), orange balls are the strangest artifacts found on power lines. But at least the orange balls, occasionally orange discs or bottles, do serve a purpose.

Power lines are thin and difficult for pilots to see. Many utility companies place balls on lines that are in the flight path of a nearby airport. After a snowstorm, the orange ball might be the only visible sign of the wires or utility poles.

We spoke to Bill Sherrard, manager of publications at Long Island Lighting in New York, who told us that his company has placed balls on their wires for another safety reason. When birds are in migration patterns, the balls let our feathered friends know where the lines are. As even nonornithologists know, birds love to perch on power lines.

Submitted by J. Melville Capps of Somerville, Massachusetts. Thanks also to Rory Sellers of Santa Fe, New Mexico; and Janice Catania of Marlboro, New York.

What Is the Purpose of the Coloring on the Toes of Some Men's Socks?

A few sock manufacturers color-code their socks so that workers at their plants can discriminate between different styles. And some predyed yarns are knitted into the sock to indicate to the seamer exactly where he or she should place the seam when the toe is closed after the sock is knitted.

But the colored toes serve primarily a marketing function. Sid Smith, president and chief executive officer of the National Association of Hosiery Manufacturers, told *Imponderables*:

> ... it is impractical, and nearly impossible, to provide a permanent label or printed information on each sock regarding its style, brand name, and other information. All of the required data is placed on the packaging, which is available to the consumer at the time and place of the retail purchase of the product. This is a reasonable and acceptable practice for the federal, state, and local regulatory agencies, and the hosiery industry, as all pertinent information is transferred to the consumer at the point of purchase.

The "packaging," usually a paper band stretched around once-folded socks, is presumably discarded by the consumer the first time he wears the socks. But if a man wears the socks for a while and likes them, how is he supposed to remember which brand they are? Often, the knitted-in coloring in the toe is the only means to identify the brand and/or the style of the socks. The phrase "they all look alike" could have been coined to describe the exasperation of the average man trying to find exactly what brand and style of black socks he bought 18 months ago.

Why do they place the coloring in the toe area rather than the heel or the ankle? Although hoity-toity designers now license their names for socks, consumers haven't yet shown a propensity for flaunting their hosiery preferences. The toe is chosen because when worn, the brand identification is well hidden from view. Smith adds that several companies do place pre-dyed colored yarns in other places on their socks, including the heel and the top band.

Submitted by Karen McNeil of Staten Island, New York. Thanks also to Kevin Olmstead of Warren, Michigan.

LET'S FACE IT—OLD ZEALAND WAS NOWHERE!

Ho-Hum!

Old Zealand

TRY New Zealand

☆ Great New Shape!
☆ Fabulous Topography!
☆ Green, Green, Green!
☆ Off that beaten path!

Where Is Old Zealand?

The first thing we did after reading this Imponderable was to laugh for an extended period of time. Then we had a brilliant idea. We looked up "Zealand" in the dictionary. We found the following: "largest island of Denmark, between Jutland and Sweden."

We remembered that the first European to land on New Zealand was Abel Tasman, a Dutchman. Now we know that all of the famous explorers blundered upon their discoveries, but this was too much. Did Tasman actually name his island after the wrong country? Was he a traitor?

Not quite. Tasman worked for the powerful Dutch East India Company, which wanted to find new trading partners willing to part with gold or silver in exchange for Dutch cloth and iron (now you know why the Dutch East India Company was successful).

Dutch explorers had already found Australia, which they called "New Holland." But they didn't realize that it was an island; the company thought that New Holland might extend south to where Antarctica is located. Abel Tasman didn't find the long continent he expected, but he and his crew were the first to discover several islands. The first was what Tasman named Van Diemen's Land (after his Governor-General)—its name was later changed to Tasmania, for obvious reasons.

Sailing east from Van Diemen's, Tasman bumped into a big land mass that, much to his consternation, was occupied by Maori tribesmen who didn't cotton to European intruders. The Maoris paddled up to the strange boats in their canoes, shouting and sounding combat trumpets. The Dutch thought they were being met by a welcoming committee and blew their trumpets back! Eventually, the Dutch did get the message when tribesmen killed several of Tasman's men and made it impossible for the crew to explore the land.

Tasman's diaries record that he named his discovery "Staten Landt." Tasman theorized that this island was actually only a small part of a great continent stretching all the way from the South Pacific to the foot of South America. So he named his discovery after Staten, the land off the southern tip of Argentina.

The very next year, another Dutchman discovered that Staten was an island and not part of South America, so Staten Landt no longer was a suitable name for Tasman's discovery. The Dutch renamed the island "Zeeland" ("sea land"), not after the Danish island but after a province of the same name back in Holland.

Probably because of the Maori's unfriendly greeting, the Dutch didn't follow up Tasman's discovery until Captain James Cook's expedition in 1769. But Tasman, one of the few explorers not to impose his name upon any of his discoveries, was later honored by having not only the island of Tasmania but a bay and a sea named after him.

Submitted by Bill Sinesky of Orrville, Ohio.

Why Do Sonic Booms Often Come Two at a Time?

Sonic booms are caused by the displacement of air around an aircraft flying faster than the speed of sound. Even slow-moving aircraft can produce pressure waves ahead of and behind the aircraft that travel at the speed of sound. But once supersonic speeds are attained, pressure disturbances called "shock waves" form behind the aircraft and reach the ground in the form of a thunderlike sound.

Many parts of the airplane are capable of creating shock waves, even the wings. But as the distance between the airplane and a person on the ground increases, only two shock waves are felt—the bow shock wave and the tail shock wave. Bill Spaniel, public information coordinator of Lockheed Aeronautical Systems Company, sent a clipping from *Above and Beyond: The Encyclopedia of Aviation and Space Sciences, Vol. II*, that explains the phenomenon:

> As the distance between the airplane and the observer is increased, the distance between the bow and tail shock waves is also increased. A person on the ground may even hear two booms, with a time interval between the bow shock wave and the tail shock wave of one-tenth to four-tenths of a second.

These shock waves pattern themselves in a cone shape, and can be felt on the ground for miles on either side of the flight path.

If you haven't noticed an increase in sonic booms since the introduction of the Concorde, the explanation is that supersonic aircraft travel at heights often twice that of subsonic widebodies. Although just as many shock waves are created at 65,000 feet altitude as at 30,000 feet, the intensity of the sonic boom is diminished by the extra mileage down to the ground.

Submitted by Dr. J. S. Hubar of Pittsburgh, Pennsylvania.

Why Are Rental Cars So Cheap in Florida?

Yes, we've heard the first rule of success in business: "Location. Location. Location." Still, on Sundays we read the travel section of the *New York Times* and wonder why it costs more to rent a car for two days in New York City than it does to rent a car for a week in Florida. Why the huge discrepancy?

We contacted some of the biggest names in car rentals—Hertz, Avis, Alamo, and Thrifty—and they spoke as one. The answer is the first rule of pricing: "Competition. Competition. Competition." According to Dick Burnon, communications manager for Hertz:

> The Sunshine State is the biggest, most competitive car-rental market in the world. Consumers benefit from this extreme competition among car-rental companies, and the result is very low rates for leisure rentals.

Notice that Burnon refers to low rates for "leisure rentals." The heavy price competition is for vacationers, so the low rates are usually reserved for weekly rentals. Business travelers, usually on expense accounts, seldom need a car for a week, and pay for the privilege with much higher per-day rates. This explains why most rental-car companies demand that you keep the car for a minimum number of days for a weekly rental—that's right, it often costs more to rent the same car from the same agency for three days than for a week. Airlines demand that Supersaver fare recipients stay over Saturday nights at their destination, a similar attempt to weed out business customers.

Phyllis Schweers, manager of Consumer Services at Thrifty Rent-A-Car Systems, complains that there is an overabundance of rental cars in southern Florida. As long as the competition is so fierce in this attractive market, and the oversupply continues, prices will be artificially low.

Other markets that feature inexpensive car rentals include Arizona, California, and Nevada. All of these places are tourist magnets that feature warm weather yearlong, ensuring that the rental market will be a 12-month a year enterprise, enabling car-rental companies to amortize the cost of buying new fleets. In cold climates, such as New England, leisure rentals plummet in winter. Regardless of price, not too many people are motivated to go on pleasure drives through Vermont in March.

The thought occurs to us that if the rental companies can afford to rent cars in Florida for less than one-half the price they are charging in New York or Boston, perhaps they are making an exorbitant profit in New York and Boston.

Try Rose Oboe Reeds

Why Does the Oboe Give Pitch to the Orchestra During Tuning?

"Tradition" echoed our sources when asked this question. But this explanation isn't sufficient. After all, before the oboe was invented, harpsichords and violins gave pitch. Are there any practical advantages to the oboe?

It turns out there are. Margaret Downie Banks, curator of The Shrine to Music Museum and Center for Study of the History of Musical Instruments in Vermillion, South Dakota, says that the oboists' double reeds "are made specifically to play at the pitch to which the orchestra will be tuning," a perfect A. The reeds are difficult to make because of their extreme rigidity. But they also are much less flexible in pitch than most instruments and less likely to waver in pitch.

The tone color of the oboe is exceptionally pure. Norman Savig, music librarian of the University of Northern Colorado, puts it this way: "the oboe has a high-pitched, clear, penetrating sound." Even the farthest-flung member of a large orchestra has no problem hearing the oboe.

High technology has invaded orchestra tuning. Acoustical experts have long contended that oboes do not supply perfect pitch. More than twenty years ago, in his book *The Acoustical Foundations of Music*, John Backus argued the point: "More reliable tuning standards than the oboe are available to orchestras willing to sacrifice tradition for accuracy in intonation."

Most big orchestras now use electronic tuners. But the oboist, in a nod to tradition, still sets the tuning bar.

Alvin Johnson, of the American Musicological Society, argues that their lack of flexibility makes oboes just as accurate as electronic tuning forks, and he adds a parting shot: "The trick isn't to get in tune. It's to play in tune."

Submitted by Dr. Amy Bug of Swarthmore, Pennsylvania. Thanks also to Manfred S. Zitsman of Wyomissing, Pennsylvania.

Why Do Newspaper Columns Give Differing Dates for the Sun Signs of the Zodiac?

Although even many of the diehard practitioners don't profess to know *why* astrology "works," this doesn't keep them from being rigorous about *how* they work. Astrologers are faced with the same dilemma as calendar makers. The year and the zodiac are divided into 12 months/signs and 365 divided by 12 simply will not yield an even number.

But the signs of the zodiac are based on the movement of the sun, a heavenly body that is much more logical in its movements than the human calendar. Astrologer Debbi Kempton-Smith told us that the exact moment of the equinoxes varies from year to year, so that the birth sign of a baby born at the exact same moment will one time be an Aquarius and another year be a Pisces.

When a newspaper column identifies the date parameters for a given sign, it means that babies born on this day in this year fall within that sun sign. To indicate a typical yearly fluctuation, Debra Burrell, of the New York School of Astrology, shared the precise moment the sun enters the sign of Pisces in three consecutive years:

> 1989: the Sun enters Pisces on February 18, 4:21 P.M., EST.
> 1990: the Sun enters Pisces on February 18, 10:15 P.M., EST.
> 1991: the Sun enters Pisces on February 19, 3:59 A.M., EST.

Like network television programming, astrologers choose to run on Eastern Standard Time.

Submitted by Panayota Karras of Huron, South Dakota.

HOW Do They Put the Holes in Macaroni and Other Pasta? Why Is Elbow Macaroni Curved?

After semolina is mixed with water and kneaded to make the wheat more smooth and elastic, the dough passes through dies —metal discs with holes. The size and shape of those holes determine what the finished pasta will look like. The National Pasta Association explains:

> Round or oval holes produce solid rods, such as linguine and spaghetti. When a steel pin is placed in the center of each hole in the die, the dough comes out in the hollow rods known as macaroni. For elbow macaroni, a pin with a notch on one side is used. The notch allows the dough to pass through more quickly on one side, causing it to curve slightly. A revolving knife attached to the die cuts the dough at frequent intervals into short lengths.

Submitted by Valerie Grollman of North Brunswick, New Jersey.

WHY DO DOGS HAVE WET NOSES?

Why Are There So Many Pins in Men's Dress Shirts and How Are They Put In?

The next time you bellyache about removing all those pins from your newly purchased dress shirt, have some compassion for the poor souls who insert them. That's right, all of those pins are stuck in by hand. If you can figure out a way to mechanize the process, you'd have some willing buyers.

So if the shirt manufacturers are willing to pay the labor expense to insert all those pins, they are not there for frivolous reasons. The main functions of the pins are to protect the shirts from damage and to enhance the appearance of the shirts at the retail level.

Many shirts, even from domestic companies, are manufactured in Asia and sent to North America in container ships, stacked collar-to-collar. The collar pins are particularly crucial to retailers, since shirts are displayed in transparent packaging and the collar is the most visually striking feature of a shirt. Customers also have a tendency to grab shirts on the rack by the collar and the pins help prop them up. Most of the pins on the body of the shirt are there to prevent the shirt from unraveling as the garment gets manhandled at the store.

We spoke to Mark Weber, corporate vice-president for marketing of Phillips-Van Heusen, who told us that a great deal of thought is put into the look and feel of what seems to be rather simple shirt packaging. For example, research indicates that the sound of the tissue paper crinkling in a shirt package is appealing to the consumer, so some companies put in the tissue, which isn't essential to preserve the shirt.

Weber adds that there is a side benefit to placing so many pins in shirts: They act as a deterrent to customers opening up the package in the store.

Submitted by Laurie Ann von Schmidt of Winsted, Connecticut. Thanks also to John F. Gwinn of Cuyahoga Falls, Ohio, and Karen and Mark Landau of Valley Cottage, New York.

Is There Any Logic to the Numbers Assigned to Boeing Jets? What Happened to the Boeing 717?

The first Boeing airplane was, appropriately enough, assigned the number 1 in the late 1910s. From then on, Boeing has grouped its product lines in series.

The first series, numbers 1-102, featured mostly biplanes. The first pressurized airplane, the Boeing 307 Stratoliner, was part of the 300 series that also included the Boeing 314 Clipper seaplane. Many military planes were included in the 200 and 400 series (the B-17 bomber was also known as the 299; B-47 and B-52 jet bombers were part of the 400 series). Boeing reserved the entire 500 series for industrial products, such as gas turbine engines. GAPA and Bomarc missiles were grouped in the 600 series.

When the prototype for the 707 jet was being designed, it

WHY DO DOGS HAVE WET NOSES?

was given a working number of 367-80. The intent was to disguise the jet as if it were just an update of the Boeing Stratocruiser. When the plane was ready to be unveiled, the 700 series was created in its honor.

Why was the first plane named the "707" instead of the "700"? According to Boeing, the name was picked

> simply because it was catchy. Since then, Boeing has built on that base of publicity and continued the naming sequence.
>
> The numbers are assigned in the order the airplane was designed, not by the number of engines or even dates of introduction. Hence the 727, which came before the 737, has three engines while the 737 has only two. The 767 was introduced into passenger service in late 1982, while the 757 came on the air transport scene in early 1983.

So what happened to the Boeing 717? Perhaps because the company didn't realize that their 7 _ 7 series would become a staple of the international aviation scene, Boeing assigned the 717 number to another jet—the KC-135, an aerial refueler produced for the United States Air Force. The Air Force still uses the 717, more than 25 years after it was introduced.

To forestall future questions—yes, 800- and 900-model series already exist, and have been assigned to such esoterica as lunar orbiters and hydrofoil boats.

Submitted by Fred Murphy of Menlo Park, California. Thanks also to David Goldsmith of Berkeley, California.

Why Do Fly Swatters Have Holes?

Elementary physics. The holes in fly swatter blades reduce wind resistance, thus increasing the velocity of the snap. The faster you snap the blade, the better your chances are of killing the varmint.

All of our varied fly-swatter experts agreed that lowering

wind resistance was the major function of blade holes, but we had a fascinating conversation with a man who dares to think even deeper thoughts. Jim Cowen is president of the world's largest manufacturer of fly swatters, Roxide International, Inc.

Roxide experiments constantly with different materials to increase blade speed. Cowen is particularly proud of his all-plastic swatter, which uses Lexan® resin, a General Electric polymer found in automobile bumpers. Lexan permits the shaft of the all-plastic swatters to "flex much like a pole vaulter's fiberglass pole would flex," increasing the chances of a quick and clean kill.

But not all of Roxide's customers prefer space-age technology. Cowen says that farmers, in particular, prefer all-metal swatters. Why?

> . . . they feel the finer mesh in the all-metal fly swatter prevents the possibility of an 'air pillow' forming underneath the swatter blade which would literally push the fly out of the way before the swatter struck.

Regardless of material preference, all fly swatter users are united in their desire for a clean kill (after all, the holes in a fly swatter were not designed to act as a strainer), and Cowen assures us that there is a secret to ensuring "swatting success."

> An individual should hold the swatter blade several feet over a fly for ten seconds or so. In this time the fly will become accustomed to having something over his head, relax his springing/escape position and start to groom his tongue and his legs [usually to eliminate food particles]. When this occurs, the fly is otherwise "engaged" and a quick flick of the wrist will kill the unsuspecting insect.

And for those of you who are too squeamish to do the dirty deed yourselves, Cowen offers a more passive solution: fly paper. Roxide invented fly paper in 1861.

Submitted by Philip Writz of Abbotsford, Wisconsin.

Why Do We Have to Send So Many of Our Magazine Subscription Orders to Boulder, Colorado?

We always thought that New York was supposed to be the publishing capital of the United States, but we'll have to reconsider. If you want a subscription to either *New York* or *The New Yorker,* the magazines that chronicle the life of our publishing capital, you have to send your check off to Boulder, Colorado.

What's going on in Boulder that we should know about? A company named Neodata Services.

Neodata's president, Kurt Burghardt, told us how Neodata landed in Boulder, Colorado. Neodata, which began in 1949, was originally a division of *Esquire.* The Smart family, who owned *Esquire,* used to vacation in Estes Park, and would drive through Boulder on their way. The Smarts figured Boulder would provide good, cheap labor. In 1963, Neodata was incorporated as a separate company, and is now owned by Dun & Bradstreet Corporation.

About half of all subscriptions are processed by the magazines themselves. Some of the biggest publishers, such as Time-Life, can achieve the economy of scale necessary to save money by processing subscriptions themselves. The other half are handled by fulfillment houses such as Neodata. Neodata is the largest subscription fulfillment house in the United States, handling over 70 million subscribers to 260 magazines, including *U.S. News and World Report, Vogue, Consumer Reports, McCalls,* and *Ski.*

Magazine fulfillment is a big business. There are 290 million subscriptions to consumer magazines; Neodata has a 22 percent share of the market but has lost the fulfillment business of *Esquire.* Neodata's next biggest competitor, Communication Data Services, located in Des Moines, Iowa, has a 17 percent share and is owned by the Hearst Corporation, which, ironically, now publishes *Esquire.*

The big fulfillment houses maintain super computers to handle the millions of orders they must process. Neodata, for example, maintains production facilities in Ireland. When you send out a subscription card to Boulder, it might be shipped with hundreds of thousands of cards to Ireland, where workers will input the data and then transmit the information back electronically to Neodata's computers in Boulder. If you order a magazine through a discount mail-order house, such as Publishers Clearinghouse or American Family, it will send your order to a fulfillment house as well.

Because most magazines who hire fulfillment houses wish to preserve the illusion that they are servicing their own subscriptions, fulfillment houses toil in obscurity and keep a low profile. You will never see Neodata's name on a subscription form or an address label, but at least you will now know why you are sending a subscription to *The New Yorker* to Boulder, Colorado.

Submitted by Steve N. Kohn of Copperas Cove, Texas. Thanks also to Dr. Seth Koch of Silver Spring, Maryland; and Jim Eason of San Francisco, California.

What's the Difference between Electric Perk and Electric Drip Coffee?

Sarah Moore, of San Francisco's Hills Brothers Coffee, assures us that the exact same coffee beans are used for both blends. The only difference is that the percolator coffee is ground coarsely, and the drip coffee is given a finer grind.

In a percolator, the brewing water and beverage is recirculated through the grounds, potentially turning the liquid into sludge. Bridget A. MacConnell, of General Foods USA, explains: "Perk coffeemakers do not use filters, so if the grind was as fine as it is for drip coffeemakers (which do use filters), you would end up with coffee grounds in your cup."

Submitted by Terry Peak of Pierce City, Missouri.

Why Do Male Dogs Lift Their Legs to Urinate?

Contrary to popular belief, the reason dogs lift their legs isn't to avoid "missing" and squirting their legs by mistake. Whenever you ask an expert any question about animal behavior, be prepared to receive the answer "to map territory." So it is with the matter of dog urination.

Most dogs are compulsive in their urination habits and have favorite "watering holes." By lifting a leg, the urine flows up and out much farther, extending the boundaries of the male's "territory." From a dog's point of view, evidently, the bigger their territory, the better.

We talked to veterinarian Ben Klein about this Imponderable and he mentioned that the lifting of the leg seems to be linked to the testicular hormone. Puppies who have been castrated before the age of four months tend not to lift their legs to urinate, with no obvious ill effect.

We then asked Dr. Klein if this mapping works. Do dogs respect the territory of other dogs? Dr. Klein responded: "Not any more than people do." In other words, male dogs, like their macho human counterparts, are indulging in flashy but ultimately futile behavior.

Submitted by Wilma Lee Sayre of Cottageville, West Virginia. Thanks also to Adam Hicks of Potomac, Maryland; Villard Brida of Weirton, West Virginia; Bob Campbell of Pullman, Washington; and Lawrence Ince of Briarwood, New York.

Why Are Television Sets Measured Diagonally?

Rarely has any Imponderable elicited such hemming and hawing. But then we found the brave man who would utter what others were merely hinting at. So we yield the floor to Scott J. Stevens, senior patent counsel for Thomson Consumer Electronics, a division of General Electric: "... the diagonal measurement is larger than either the horizontal or vertical measurement, hence making the picture appear as large as possible to potential customers."

Submitted by John D. Claypoole, Jr. of Norwalk, Connecticut. Thanks also to Mike Ricksgers of Saxonburg, Pennsylvania.

AMY NEESIA
61 Ave. of Oblivion
Recollection, OH 00??0

101

PAY _Through the Nose, Inc._ $ _1000 00_

One Thousand — but, hey, wait a Second xx/xx

What happened to my first 100 checks ?!! _Puzzled_

When You Order Checks from a Bank, Why Is the First Check Numbered "101" Rather Than "1"?

We always assumed that the first check is numbered "101" because no one wants to cash a check numbered "1." It would be the financial equivalent of showing up in high school with lily-white sneakers or unbroken-in jeans.

And there is something to this theory. Fred Burgerhoff, of Deluxe Check Printers, told _Imponderables_ that many businesses request checks starting with 1001 or 10,001, since no concern wants a customer or associate to think it just opened its doors.

Many individuals don't realize that they can also request their checks to start with any number they want. Some merchants are reluctant to cash checks with low numbers. Deluxe's Stuart Alexander remembers the days when many merchants put up signs stating they would not cash checks below number 500.

David Taylor, of the Bank Administration Institute, says that merchants and banks have good reason to be wary of new accounts. More than half of all check frauds occur within the first 90 days of an account being established. Taylor adds that most banks institute special procedures for scrutinizing checking accounts during this 90-day period, monitoring for suspicious deposits or withdrawals that might indicate a kiting operation.

Even if bank customers preferred their checks to start with "1," the check printers and banks would rather give them "101" instead. Stuart Alexander says that the numbering machines used by printers have a minimum setting of three digits, so that checks would have to read "001" rather than "1."

When you open a checking account, it takes several weeks before personalized checks can be issued, so you are given a starter kit including several unnumbered checks. But for bookkeeping purposes, banks don't want the numbers on personalized checks to conflict with numbers assigned by customers to the starter-kit checks.

Submitted by Jon R. Kennedy of Charlotte, North Carolina.

Why Won't or Why Can't One-hour Photo Developers Process Black-and-White Film in One Hour?

They could. But there isn't enough demand to make it a profitable enterprise.

But help may be at hand. Ilford's XP-1 black and white film can be processed by many one-hour color labs. According to Thomas J. Dufficy, of the National Association of Photographic Manufacturers, although they may not advertise it, many developers can print XP-1 on black and white paper in one hour, using the same equipment they do for color film.

Submitted by Nils Montag of Chicago, Illinois. Thanks also to Jena Mori of Los Angeles, California.

Do Submarines Have Anchors?

They sure do. Submarines need anchors for the same reason that other ships do. Any time a submarine needs to maintain its position on the surface but doesn't happen to be near a pier or another vessel, the anchor is used. Anchors aren't needed while submarines are submerged, but subs have to resurface sometime, so anchors come in handy.

One of our favorite correspondents, George Flower, who happens to be in the navy, wrote to us: "A submarine on the surface is a very unstable platform, as any sub sailor will be willing to tell you." We were under the misapprehension that an anchor would help stabilize a submarine, but Captain G. L. Graveson, Jr., public affairs director of the Naval Submarine League, disabused us of the notion. Captain Graveson told *Imponderables* that in a rough sea with the anchor down, the ship will tend to position itself perpendicular to the wind; to this extent, an anchor might help cut turbulence on the surface.

But Graveson claims that submarines aren't noticeably more unstable on the surface than other ships. He noted that the worst instability on a submarine is usually experienced in the process of diving or resurfacing; as the centers of gravity and bouyancy change, so do the complexions of some of the queasier sailors.

Submitted by Jim Kowald of Green Bay, Wisconsin.

Why Are There No Photographs in the *Wall Street Journal?*

On rare occasions there *are* photographs in the *Wall Street Journal,* but it is safe to say that if Clark Kent had worked for *WSJ* instead of the *Daily Planet,* Jimmy Olsen wouldn't have been Superman's confidant.

The *Wall Street Journal* was designed as a financial broadsheet and has never had an official policy against photographs. When it profiles a pillar of finance, the *Journal* usually illustrates the article with a dot drawing of the subject. But if an editor decides that a photograph is necessary to enhance the story, a photograph is included. Decades of tradition make it unlikely that an editor casually will order a photograph—the *Wall Street Journal* has never hired a staff photographer.

The first issue of the *Wall Street Journal* rolled off the presses on July 8, 1889; its first photograph appeared in 1927, when the obituary of the *Wall Street Journal*'s own drama critic and editor, James S. Metcalfe, was accompanied by a photograph of a painting of Metcalfe. Two years later, a photograph of an architectural sketch was printed. Not until later in 1929, when a photograph of William Hamilton accompanied his obituary, did the *Journal* print a portrait photograph.

In celebration of the fiftieth anniversary of its parent company, Dow Jones, precedent was broken and several photographs were inserted into one issue of the *Journal*. But after this burst of exuberance, photographs have appeared only intermittently, perhaps most often in obituaries. Occasionally a major world figure rates a photograph, such as Mao Tse-tung in 1976, but just as likely the honor will go to lesser subjects. The last photograph printed in the *Journal* was of Mary Alice Williams, Maria Shriver, and Chuck Scarborough, upon the premiere of their late, unlamented newsmagazine, "Yesterday, Today & Tomorrow."

Submitted by Steve Thompson of La Crescenta, California.

What Is the Purpose of the Yellow "VIOLATION" Flag Found on Parking Meters? When, if Ever, Does It Pop Up?

Any time we put a coin in a parking meter and turn the handle, the yellow "VIOLATION" flag appears, only to recede when our time is credited. On a bad day, the red "TIME EXPIRED" flag pops up if we haven't made it back to the car on time. And on a really bad day, a parking enforcement officer will notice the red flag and we will get a ticket.

But what is the need for a yellow "VIOLATION" flag when the red one signals an overtime charge? The yellow flag is there to signal the meter enforcement person that the meter is malfunctioning. If a coin gets jammed in a slot, or a driver tries to insert a foreign object into the slot, the yellow flag will not retract. While he or she is issuing tickets, the enforcement officer will notify a repair technician, who will either repair the meter on the spot or replace the mechanism with one that functions correctly.

Why does the yellow flag say "VIOLATION"? According to Dennis W. Staggs, manager of customer service at parking meter manufacturer, POM Incorporated, "City statutes make it a violation to park at a meter with the violation flag up, and in most cases, you will receive a ticket if you do park there."

Often, one can see drivers propping notes under their windshield wipers or surrounding parking meters with pieces of paper whining about how they would simply *love* to be able to put all sorts of money into the meter if only the contraption would cooperate. Little do they know that if the yellow flag is up on the meter, they have violated the law not only by inserting money into the meter but by parking in that spot in the first place.

Folks have been trying to "beat" parking meters since the early 1950s, when they first appeared in the United States. William L. Kemp, manager of international sales administration at Duncan Industries, the largest manufacturers of parking control systems in the world, has been in the industry for 38 years, and explains how nefarious types have tried to circumvent the trusty yellow flag:

> In the early years of parking meters, motorists learned that if they put their coin into the meter and only partially turned the handle, ∴ the red flag would go down and the yellow flag would come up. They would park for a longer period of time than their coin purchase allowed, assuming the enforcement officer would think the motorist just forgot to turn the handle all of the way. The officer would turn the handle to prove to himself that there was in fact a coin in the coin handler. The coin then would drop and time would wind on the meter and the motorist gained all the extra time from when he parked the car until the time the officer pulled the handle!
>
> As the practice of partially turning the handle grew as motorists became aware of the method to cheat the city, it became necessary to post labels on the meters saying "POLICE WILL NOT TURN HANDLE," and from that time on, tickets were issued to the offenders and the practice died a natural death.

What interests us is that although one of the main purposes of the "VIOLATION" flag is to deter folks from parking in a given spot, few people understand the purpose of the yellow flag. We asked twenty-five people what the purpose of the yellow flag was. Not one knew the correct answer.

Submitted by Charles Myers of Ronkonkoma, New York.

Why Don't Woodpeckers Get Headaches?

Not a bad question, especially considering that we humans have no problem contracting migraines from metaphorically beating our heads against the walls. Luckily for woodpeckers, their entire bodies are designed to peck with impunity.

Although anatomical features differ among different species of woodpeckers, all of them have unusually thick skulls. But the species that peck most frequently have a special advantage: Their skull curves inward at the upper base of the bill so that the skull is not attached to the bill. Although their beaks can withstand the frequent hammering, the separation between the bill and the skull acts as a natural shock absorber.

Actually, the bills of woodpeckers are not nearly as fragile as they appear. Yes, the tip of the bill is narrow, but it is broad-based and remarkably sturdy; the pointed tip acts as a chisel.

If anything, the biggest danger to woodpeckers is flying debris, but Mother Nature has taken care of this problem, too.

Woodpeckers' nostrils are narrow slits so that flying wood chips won't land in their noses.

Submitted by Reverend Harry T. Rowe of Milton, West Virginia.

Why Do Electronics and Automobile Repair Shops Have Such Big Backlogs? Why Don't They Hire More Repair Technicians to Reduce Their Backlogs?

This syllogism seems indisputable:

1. If you need to repair your car (say, for body work) or a busted VCR, you are going to have to wait a long time for the privilege.
2. Repair work is a highly profitable business.
3. Therefore, it is in the self-interest of repair shops to do more repairs.

Sure, it costs money for repair shops to hire more technicians or add work benches (about $20,000 for a modern audio workbench and many times that for an automobile mechanic's bay), but isn't it cost-effective to add capacity when backlogs are so consistently high? Furthermore, a good facility that could also perform repairs quickly would gain more business simply because of the quick turnaround.

Surely, the repair industries must have thought these issues through. So why does it still take two weeks to get a repair done? According to Richard L. Glass, president of the Professional Electronics Technicians Association, the problem is that the public won't pay for added costs entailed in fast service. Obviously, any service business that guarantees immediate (or even same-day) repairs will by necessity have technicians idle at non-peak periods or technicians unqualified to perform particularly difficult repairs. Glass elaborates:

> We pay for ambulance drivers and firemen to sit and wait for accidents and fires. We don't pay for technicians to sit and wait

for higher than average incidences of service, or peaks in service demand. We find the public is outraged at $50 per hour labor fees by electronics technicians working on consumer products, yet IBM and Xerox technicians must charge $125+ on their calls, when in fact the consumer technician has a much more difficult job.

Sometimes repair facilities try to expand and meet resistance. John Loftus, of the Society of Collision Repair Specialists, told us that many communities won't give zoning clearances for collision repair facilities, so that even successful shops with good locations can't expand to handle increased business.

Mike Zazanas, of the Professional Audio Retailers Association, told *Imponderables*, with more than a little frustration, that in the repair industry the shops that have big backlogs tend to have the best technicians. Zazanas told us that if several qualified technicians walked into his store as he was speaking to us, he'd offer them jobs (and presumably put us on hold). But "it's impossible to find one." In the "old days," entry-level technicians were "screwdriver mechanics" or "tube jerkers" who simply replaced and tested tubes. With the advent of transistors, electronics, and chips, even lower-level technicians must have a higher level of education and expertise.

The crux of the problem, according to John Loftus, is more sociological than economic. Now that a formal education is necessary to become an electronics technician, most prospective technicians decide in school to become electronic engineers instead. Even though, in most cases, they would make as much money fixing equipment as designing it, engineering conjures up visions of white collars while technical work means blue collars and grimy hands. To many, a white collar means creativity and prestige; a blue collar signifies monotony and lack of education. Until this prejudice against technical work is combated, Loftus thinks the problem of attracting talented technicians will persist.

Because the space requirements of an electronics repair shop are more modest, everyone in the industry we contacted

WHY DO DOGS HAVE WET NOSES?

said that the major factor causing backlogs is a lack of qualified technicians. If they could find the technicians, retailers would gladly hire them.

The car repair picture is spottier. We contacted each of the Big Three automakers in the U.S., and none professed concern about a problem with the waiting time for repairs. Why should they add new bays to their service facilities when the new equipment is so expensive and, evidently, few are complaining to them about waiting a week to get a tune-up.

Why Does Sound Linger for a Few Seconds After You Unplug a Radio?

Dick Glass, president of the Professional Electronics Technicians Association, took a few minutes away from his repair backlog to give us the answer to this Imponderable:

> Sound lingers because filter capacitors charge up to the power supply voltage level, say 24 volts. The filter capacitors are extremely large so that any ripples in the power line voltage, or surges, will be smoothed out.
> Turning off the radio still leaves the capacitors charged up. Until the transistors or bleed-off circuits lower that voltage, the radio continues to operate as if it were connected to a battery. If you had a filter capacitor large enough, you could operate the radio for hours without it being plugged in and turned on.

Submitted by Dr. Charles Waggoner of Macomb, Illinois.

Why Are Three Consecutive Strikes in Bowling Called a "Turkey"?

"Turkey" has long been a favorite research project for word experts. Many books on etymology will go on at length about how a North American bird was named after a country in which it has never existed. They will speculate about how "talking turkey" originated.

But two of the stranger uses of "turkey" are not clearly documented. Although disparaging uses of "turkey" have existed since the nineteenth century, no one seems to know why the word came to describe a show business flop.

We've also been unable to find any written reference to the origin of the bowling term. But Mark Gerberich, director of operations of the Professional Bowlers Association, passed on the thoughts of PBA historian Chuck Pezzano, who knows as much as anyone about the subject:

> There used to be sweepstake tournaments during the holidays, Christmas and Thanksgiving. If a person bowled three strikes

against the heavier pins (usually four pounds), the crowd would scream "turkey" and the bowler would receive a live turkey for his or her performance.

Submitted by Elizabeth Skomp of Crawfordsville, Indiana.
Thanks also to Carlos F. Lima of Middletown, Wisconsin.

Why Is Teddy Roosevelt Always Depicted Charging up San Juan Hill When There Were No Horses in Cuba During the Spanish-American War?

The poser of this Imponderable, Herb Clark, adds that there was no room for horses in the ships that took Roosevelt and his men to Cuba. So why this flight of fantasy by artists?

As much as we hate to quibble with a reader, we must make one amendment to your premise, Herb. True, there wasn't room on the ships to transport horses for the regiment. But there was room for the horses of a few key officers. Roosevelt's horse, Texas, was shipped to Cuba and Teddy did indeed ride the horse in the battle of San Juan Hill.

Submitted by Herb Clark of Hopkins, Minnesota.

Why Don't Planets Twinkle at Night?

What causes a heavenly body to twinkle? Alan MacRobert, of astronomy magazine *Sky & Telescope*, explains:

> Twinkling is caused by light rays being diverted slightly—jiggled around—by turbulence where warm and cool air mixes in the upper atmosphere. One moment a ray of light from the star will hit your eye; the next moment, it misses.

Our eyes fool our brains into thinking that the star is jumping around in the sky.

Stars are so far away from us that even when viewed through a sophisticated telescope, they look like single points of light. Even though planets may at first appear the same size as stars to the naked eye, they are actually little disks in the sky. Jeff Kanipe, associate editor of *Astronomy*, told *Imponderables* that "the disks of planets like Venus, Mars, Jupiter, and Saturn can be easily seen by looking at them with a pair of binoculars or a small telescope."

How does this difference in size between stars and planets affect their "twinkling quotient"? We've already established that stars appear to the eye as single points. Kanipe explains how that one point turns into a twinkle:

> When starlight passes through about 200 miles of Earth's atmosphere, the light-bending properties of the different layers of air act like lenses that bend and jiggle the rays to such an extent that the star's position appears to jump about very slightly, causing it to twinkle.

MacRobert contrasts the effect of refraction upon our view of a planet:

> The disk of a planet can be regarded as many points packed close together [yes, like a thousand points of light]. When one point twinkles bright for a moment another may be faint. The differences average out and their combined light appears steady.

Kanipe phrases it a little differently:

> A planet's light comes from every part of its disk, not just a single point. Thus, when the light passes through the atmosphere, the shift in position is smaller than the size of the planet's disk in the sky and the twinkling isn't as pronounced.

Still don't get it? Let's use a more down-to-earth analogy, supplied by Kanipe:

> From the vantage point of a diving board, a dime on the floor of the swimming pool appears to shift violently about because the water acts like a wavy lens that continuously distorts the rays of light coming from the coin. But a submerged patio table, say, looks fairly steady because the water can't distort the light rays coming from its greater surface area to the point that the table appears to shift out of position.

Submitted by Henry J. Stark of Montgomery, New York. Thanks also to Frank H. Anderson of Prince George, Virginia, and J. Leonard Hiebert of Nelson, British Columbia.

Why Do We Wake Up with Bad Breath in the Morning?

Most bad breath (or "fetid breath," as dentists like to call it) is caused by sulfur-bearing compounds in the mouth. How do they get there? And why is the problem worse in the morning?

Microorganisms in the mouth aren't fussy about what they eat. They attack:

Food left in the mouth.

Plaque.

Saliva found in the spaces between teeth, the gum, and on the tongue.

Dead tissue that is being shed by the mouth, gums, and tongue.

The microorganisms convert this food into amino acids and peptides, which in turn break down into compounds with a pungent sulfur odor.

Brushing the teeth helps rid the mouth of all of these food sources of the microorganisms. But the best defense is a regular salivary flow, the type you get by talking, chewing, or swallowing—the stuff that most of us do only when awake.

Eliminating cavities is not the only reason to floss. The longer food particles stay in the mouth, the more fetid the breath will be, so those six to ten hours of sleep are the perfect breeding time for bacteria and a threat to sensitive noses everywhere.

Submitted by Rowena Nocom of North Hollywood, California; Thanks also to Jason Glass of El Monte, California, and Richard Slonchka of McKees Rock, Pennsylvania.

How Do Carbonated Soft Drink Manufacturers Manage to Fill Bottles without Spilling Liquid?

Not all bottling methods work in exactly the same way, but the following scenario is typical.

Empty bottles are lifted on a platform that rises up to meet a filler. The fill height is preset by adjusting vent tubes on the filler. Margie Spurlock, manager of consumer affairs for Royal Crown Cola, explains it:

> These vent tubes have small holes in the side which are closed except for the one at the desired fill height. Beverage replaces air in the bottle as the air escapes through the vent tube hole. When the beverage covers the hole in the vent tube, the pressure is equalized and no more beverage is dispensed into the container.

Steve Del Priore, a plant manager at Pepsi-Cola's Brooklyn, New York, bottling facility, reports that no head forms on the liquid whatsoever. CO_2 is introduced as the liquid goes in the bottle so that the pressure is equalized. When the filler platform rises, a sealing rubber is put on that eliminates spillage.

Del Priore adds that the bottle caps, which are called "closures" in the soda trade, don't have threads until after they are applied; the sides of the closures are straight. But the aluminum is then stretched down with 500 pounds of pressure and small wheels shape the caps to insure that the bottle stays closed.

Submitted by Thomas I. Himmelheber of Abingdon, Maryland.

What Is the Purpose of Cigar Bands? Do They Serve Any Function Besides Advertising the Name of the Manufacturer?

The cigar band was introduced in 1854 by Gustave Bock, a European who emigrated to Cuba and helped develop the Cuban cigar industry. According to Norman F. Sharp, president of the Cigar Associates of America, Inc.:

> Bock began putting them on his cigars in 1854 in order to prevent them from being counterfeited. It seems that dealers in the days before bands would sometimes open his boxes and substitute inferior cigars for the Bock cigars.

A probably apocryphal story claims that the cigar band was developed to answer the complaints of the upper-class ladies of Cuba, who then freely smoked cigars but were bothered by the nicotine stains on their fingers. Another plausible theory suggests that the band helped keep the cigar wrapper intact in case the gum on the ends wasn't sufficient.

Today, of course, the cigar band's sole purpose is to advertise the manufacturer of the cigar, and many people collect bands as a hobby. Devotees of the stogie have long argued over whether the band should be removed when one smokes the cigar. In his book *The Cigar*, Z. Davidoff votes for removing the band but strikes a balanced tone:

> Sensitive as I am to this poetry of the band, I do recommend removing it after lighting the cigar, that is, after having smoked about a fifth of the cigar . . . the cigar is even more attractive in its nudity . . .
>
> If you prefer to smoke a cigar without its band to the halfway point or even three-quarters, go right ahead. It is not an offensive practice, and don't be upset by those who reproach you.

In these days of antismoking sentiment, being reproached for leaving on the cigar band is the least of a cigar smoker's worries.

Submitted by Douglas Watkins, Jr. of Hayward, California.

Why Is Easter Observed on Such Wildly Different Dates?

We don't know the exact day when Jesus was born or what day of the week the first Thanksgiving was observed (*see* "Why is the American Thanksgiving on Thursday?"), but at least we know when to expect to see them on our calendar every year. Easter's date varies so much because the timing of Easter is based on the lunar calendar.

Early Christians celebrated Easter on the same date as the Jewish Passover, but Christians, wanting to distance themselves from Jewish practices, changed the time of observance at the Council of Nicaea in A.D. 325. Like legislators everywhere, the Council was prone to pass some pretty complicated laws: Easter was henceforth to be celebrated on the first Sunday after the first full moon on or after the spring equinox (March 21).

Long before the resurrection of Jesus was celebrated, virtually every Western society celebrated the rebirth of nature in the spring. Ironically, one of the holiest Christian holidays is named after a pagan goddess. The name "Easter" derives from the Anglo-Saxon goddess Eostre, who governed the vernal equinox.

Submitted by Marilyn B. Atkinson of Grass Valley, California. Thanks also to Mojo Chan of Scarborough, Ontario, and Susan E. Watson of Jamestown, Rhode Island.

Why Do the Agitators in Washing Machines Go Back and Forth Rather than Spin 360 Degrees?

In order to loosen dirt from soiled laundry, the clothes must move in the machine. If the agitator spun continuously, centrifugal force would actually make the clothes stick in one spot. So the back and forth movement of most top-loading washing machine agitators actually moves the clothes more.

Submitted by Gabrielle Popoff of Rancho Santa Fe, California.

Why Do Most Hotels and Motels Place Exactly Three Sets of Towels in the Bathroom Regardless of the Number of Beds or Persons in the Room?

We've observed that most hotel/motel towel racks are designed to house two sets of towels. In most cases, the third set of towels is slung over the other two.

Why do innkeepers bother with the extra towels when the vast majority of rooms are occupied by one or two persons? James P. McCauley, executive director of the International As-

WHY DO DOGS HAVE WET NOSES?

sociation of Holiday Inns, Inc., was kind enough to survey some hotel owners for us. This is what he heard:

> The answer seems to be seasonal or dependent on the availability of an indoor/outdoor pool or whirlpool. Most hotels/motels that have outdoor pools offer extra towels during the summer. Those hotels that offer an indoor swimming pool or whirlpool could have an extra set of towels in the room during the entire year. The more amenities offered, the more likely a third set of towels, or at least an extra-large towel.

We also heard from Richard M. Brooks, vice-president of rooms management at Stouffer Hotels and Resorts. In its resort properties, Stouffer actually requires four sets of towels in each room because most rooms are occupied by two people who will each likely need one towel for a bath and the other for a post-swim shower.

But most commercial hotels cater to single travelers. Brooks says that fewer than 25 percent of Stouffer's nonresort hotels are occupied by more than one person at a time. So hotels want to put in the fewest possible number of towels in each room. The expense can add up:

> By providing only three towels, hotels keep their investment in towels to a minimum. Remember, most good hotels keep three to four times the number of terry and linen items necessary in stock to be sure guests have a sufficient supply. In a typical Stouffer property, this usually means an investment of well over $250,000.

Submitted by Charles Myers of Ronkonkoma, New York.

Why Are Peaches Fuzzy?

We heard from about fifteen experts on peaches, all of whom agreed that the fuzz is there for a reason. Exactly what that reason is was considerably harder to nail down.

Perhaps the best consensus answer was provided by Charles D. Kesner, horticulturist at Michigan State University's College of Agriculture and Natural Sciences:

> Peaches are in the Rose family, genus Prunus, specie persica. Peach fuzz is genetic and likely selectively developed to give the fruit more resistance to insects and diseases. Although peach fruits do sustain some disease and insect damage, they are much more resistant than the nectarine which was developed by plant breeders with recessive genes for the fuzzless character. Therefore, a nectarine is simply a peach without fuzz.

Want some other theories?

The California Cling Peach Advisory Board adds that the fuzz also protects peaches from sunburn.

Clay Weeks, a peach specialist in the pomology department at the University of California, Davis, mentions that fuzz helps reduce potential water loss in the fruit.

Davis plant pathologist Dr. Joe Ogawa mentions that fuzz not only helps collect rain water for the fruit but also serves as a barrier against fungus as well as insects.

Perhaps the best evidence that nature provided fuzz for functional reasons is the contrast between peaches and its fuzz-less brother, the nectarine. Nectarines are far less sturdy than peaches. They are more susceptible to brown rot and tend to be bruised in transit more easily than fuzzy peaches.

Why Can't You Buy Canned Nectarines?

Fresh nectarines are a popular commodity. And we just learned that nectarines are essentially fuzzless peaches (with the difference of one recessive gene). So is there a technical reason why it is hard to can nectarines? Or is it a matter of lack of demand?

A little bit of both, it turns out. Only one person we contacted, Les Rose, vice president of operations for the Apricot Producers of California, claimed that nectarines can as well as freestone peaches. Rose contends that a lack of demand (as well as the higher prices fetched by fresh product) is responsible for the lack of canned nectarines.

But our other sources felt that technical considerations were more important. Nectarines tend to be very soft. Bill Johnson, manager of Information Services for the California Canning Peach Association, says that the mechanical processing required for canned fruits tends to ruin the texture of nectarines. The fruit bruises easily, leading to a poor appearance.

Ronald A. Schuler, president of the California Canning Peach Association, says that a processor in Fresno, California, tried to can nectarines several years ago but couldn't avoid severe losses in yield because of the soft fruit.

The supply of nectarines also tends to be less bountiful than peaches. According to Charles D. Kesner, horticulturist at Michigan State University's Northwest Michigan Horticultural Experiment Station, nectarines are highly susceptible to brown rot. The expense of eliminating brown rot in humid climates is not worth the cost, so domestic production of nectarines is confined to the western United States.

Ronald A. Schuler says that "the canning of regular yellow fleshed freestones is also moving toward extinction in the retail can sizes." As consumers increasingly opt for fresh produce, the bucks for the growers are in fresh rather than canned product.

Submitted by Douglas Watkins, Jr. of Hayward, California.

Why Do Dogs Love to Put Their Heads Out the Windows of Moving Cars? But Then Hate to Have Their Ears Blown Into?

Most of the people who have asked this Imponderable connect these two questions, wondering why a dog loves speeding down a freeway at 65 MPH (with its head totally exposed to the wind) when it balks at a little playful ear blowing. But dog authorities insisted the two Imponderables we were talking about mixed apples and oranges.

Of course, nobody has been able to interview canines on the subject, but the consensus is that dogs like to put their heads out of car windows because they are visually curious. Many dogs are not tall enough to have an unobstructed view of the outside world from the front seat, and most dogs are too short to have any forward or rearward view from the back seat. Poking their

WHY DO DOGS HAVE WET NOSES?

head out of the window is a good way to check out their sur-
roundings and enjoy a nice, cool breeze at the same time.

But blowing in a dog's ear, even gently, can hurt it, not
because of the softness of the skin or the sensitivity of the nerves,
but because of the sound of the blowing. Veterinarian Ben Klein
told *Imponderables* that one of the ways a dog is tested for deafness is by the vet blowing into the ear through a funnel; if the
dog doesn't get upset, it's an indication of deafness. So while we
may associate blowing into the ear of a dog as playfulness or to a
human mate as a sexual overture, to the dog it is the canine
equivalent of scratching a blackboard with fingernails. The frequency of the sound drives them nuts.

Dr. William E. Monroe, of the American College of Veterinary Internal Medicine, adds that the external ears of dogs are
full of sensory nerves that help to prevent trauma injuries and
preserve hearing:

> By preventing debris (sand, wood chips, etc.) from entering the
> ear canal, damage to the ear and hearing is prevented. Thus,
> avoiding air in the ear could have survival advantage.

The ear can't trap all the debris a dog must contend with. In
fact, Dr. Klein mentioned that sticking their heads out of car
windows is one of the major causes of ear infections in dogs.

Next thing we know, we'll have to install seat belts for dogs.

*Submitted by Frederick A. Fink of Coronado, California. Thanks
also to Allison Crofoot of Spring Valley, New York; Rich
Williams of San Jose, California; Candace Savalas of New York,
New York; Douglas Watkins, Jr. of Hayward, California;
Melanie Jongsma of Lansing, Illinois; Jacob Schneider of
Norwalk, Ohio; David Hays and Paul Schact of Newark, Ohio;
and Roseanne Vitale of Port St. Lucie, Florida.*

Why Do Many Brands of Aspirin Not Have a Safety Cap on Their 100-Count Bottles?

The Poison Packaging Act of 1970 mandated that if the contents of any packaged substance could pose a significant hazard to children, and if it is technically feasible, the package must contain a safety cap. Most of us have gotten used to trying to align those two confounded arrows and trying to exert enough leverage to flip the cap off. But if you don't have long fingernails, it's hard to get leverage; and if you have long fingernails, you don't have long fingernails for long.

A casual survey at our local drugstore reveals that the poser of this Imponderable was right. Many brands of aspirin have safety caps on all their sizes except the 100-count. What gives?

If we have problems opening the safety caps, you can imagine the problems that the elderly or sufferers of arthritis might have. So one of the provisions of the Poison Packaging Act authorized manufacturers to market one (but no more than one) size of packaging that did not comply with the safety-cap standard, as long as the package is conspicuously labeled with the words: "This package for Households Without Young Children."

Why have most aspirin marketers chosen the 100-count container for their noncomplying package? It's the most popular size. And although no one will say it on the record, we got the distinct impression that there are some nonelderly, nondisabled consumers who don't love the safety cap. By putting the easier-to-open cap on their most popular size, the companies ensure that their product will be competitive with other brands.

Thanks to Jean, a caller on the Ray Briem show, KABC-AM, Los Angeles, California.

Where Do Butterflies Go When It Rains?

Butterflies don't just prefer sunny days. They need sunlight in order to regulate their body temperature. Whether it is raining or not, when the sun is obscured or the sun sets, butterflies fly for cover immediately.

Just as human beings might duck for cover underneath the canopy of a tree, butterflies seek the protection of natural coverings. According to Rudi Mattoni, editor of the *Journal of Research on the Lepidoptera,* the favorite resting sites include the undersides of leaves or stems of bushes and on blades of grass.

Butterfly bodies are exceedingly delicate, so nature has provided them with other kinds of protection against the rain. When resting, the teardrop configuration of the butterfly prevents rain from pooling on the wings or body, and the surfaces of the butterfly's skin do not absorb water.

Richard Zack, curator/director of the James Entomological Collection at Washington State University, adds that many butterflies could not survive flying during a rainstorm. Not only does wind wreak havoc with their ability to fly, but the big raindrops themselves would pose a major risk.

Submitted by Jennifer Martz of Pottstown, Pennsylvania.

Why Do You Sometimes Find Coffee Bags Hung on the Coat Hooks of Airplane Lavatory Doors?

Flight attendants do not take grounds out of cans to brew coffee for inflight service. They simply pop in bags, which look like huge tea bags, into the coffeemaker. Although more expensive, the coffee bags totally eliminate the potential problem of runaway coffee grounds if the flight attendant were to drop a can or the plane were to experience sudden turbulence. But why must the airline, or the flight attendants, hang these bags on the coat hooks of lavatory doors, as we have seen more and more of late?

We received two different answers to this Imponderable. The first comes from an expert on airplane food service, Phillip S. Cooke, Executive Administrator of Inflight Food Service Association:

> Consider the poor, harried flight attendant who often has to serve a fairly complicated meal service in a very short time and in a very confined space (the galley was not uppermost in the minds of aircraft designers!). Sometimes the only place to hang anything, and the only hook available during these rush periods is, you guessed it, that little hook just around the corner, or across from the galley—in the lavatory. The attendants certainly mean to retrieve the coffee bags at the conclusion of service, but they also sometimes forget.

A good theory, but this is one Imponderable for which we could indulge in hands-on research. Every time we encountered coffee bags on coat hooks, we asked the flight attendants why. And we got the same answer over and over again.

As Phillip Cooke mentioned, in most nonwidebody planes, the coach galley is located at the rear of the plane, and lavatories are always nearby. Lavatories have a nasty habit of not smelling too great. Ingenious flight attendants hit upon a home remedy: coffee bags. Unused coffee grounds deodorize the lavatories for the comfort of the flight attendants and the passengers.

Airlines have to tread a thin line in treating the problem of smelly lavatories. Room deodorizers can be noxious in a big room, let alone in a tiny space without windows or good ventilation. Some airlines have chosen to use mild deodorizers, so flight attendants have been hanging coffee bags in self-defense.

Submitted by Charles Myers of Ronkonkoma, New York.

Why Is There No Interstate Number 1, 2, or 3 in the United States? Why Do You So Seldom See Highway 3s? Is There any Logical System to the Numbering of the Highway System?

Contrary to popular belief, interstate highways in the U.S. do not necessarily connect two different states. The criteria for roadways in the interstate system have more to do with technical requirements, such as the access to the highway (interstates must have totally public access), shoulders on both sides of the road, minimum width of lanes, etc.

Reader Mike Osenga is correct. The lowest-numbered interstate highway is 4, which connects Tampa and Daytona Beach in Florida, a distance of less than 150 miles. Interstate highway 5 runs up the entire west coast, from San Diego, California, to the Washington/Canadian border. What happened to numbers 1, 2, and 3?

The powers that be, namely the American Association of State Highway and Transportation Officials (AASHTO), determined that the principal north-south interstate routes should bear numbers divisible by five. Interstate highway 4, then, is the lowest even companion number to 5. Of course, even-numbered interstates run in an east-west direction, and odd-numbered ones in a north-south orientation.

But there are more rules to the numbering system than that. The lower odd numbers, such as Interstate 5, are located in the West and the lower even numbers in the South. Note that Interstate 10 runs through the southern United States, while numbers 90 and 94 cross the northern areas.

U.S. highways may duplicate the numbers already used for interstates, and odd and even numbers still indicate north-south and east-west routes, respectively. But strangely enough, the lower odd numbers are in the East (such as U.S. 1, which hugs the east coast) and the higher odd numbers, such as the Pacific Coast Highway, U.S. 101, are in the West.

Why is there a dearth of highway 3s? Although there may be no Interstate 3, there is a U.S. highway 3, which starts in New Hampshire, just south of Chartierville, Quebec, and meanders south to Boston, Massachusetts; but at 279 miles, it is one of the shortest U.S. highways. In fact, all the numbers between 1 and 27 have been taken for U.S. highways; 88 out of the first hundred numbers have been assigned. The highest U.S. highway number? 730.

The numbering of state highways isn't even this organized. Many states have even-numbered north-south routes and odd-numbered east-west highways. And if you pore over an atlas, you will notice that many states have no highway 3 or an inconspicuous highway 3. Why has 3 been singled out for obscurity and ignominy? All the sources we contacted indicated it was just a coincidence. Given the hodgepodge of numbering systems, we believe it.

Submitted by Mike Osenga of Brookfield, Wisconsin. Thanks also to William L. Chesser of Littleton, Colorado, and Tom Pietras of Battle Creek, Michigan.

Why Are There Expiration Dates on Fire Extinguishers?

No, the chemicals found in most portable fire extinguishers won't "spoil" like milk if left in past the expiration date. But according to Bill Fabricino, of BRK Electronics, "since most fire extinguishers use a pressurized gas for a propellant, the gas eventually will leak out through seals and render the extinguisher useless."

Submitted by Herbert Kraut of Forest Hills, New York.

Why Do Eyes Sometimes Come out Red in Photographs? Why Is This Particularly True of Cats' and Dogs' Eyes?

Have you ever seen "red-eye" in a professional's photographs? Of course not, because they know that paying customers want a portrait of the topography of their faces, not an intrusive journey into the blood vessels of their eyes.

Yes, the red you see is blood, and you get more red than you ever wanted to see because your flash bulb or flash cube is too close to the camera lens. Ralph E. Venk, president of the Photographic Society of America, says that the light from the flash "enters the lens of the eye directly and is then reflected off the back surface of the eyeball, the retina, and bounces back to the camera. The problem of red-eye is compounded because flashes are used in dark environments and the human eye automatically opens wider in the dark.

A few simple tips should banish red-eye from your lives:

1. Try holding the flash farther away from the lens axis. An extra three inches should do. Thomas J. Dufficy, of the National Association of Photographic Manufacturers, says that when camera makers noticed the problem with red-eye when flash

cubes were first introduced, they offered flash cube extenders, three-inch high posts that increased the angle between the camera lens axis and the flash cube.

2. When taking photographs in the dark, don't have subjects look straight into the camera. Notice that in group shots, the red-eye victim is always the one looking straight into the lens. Your subjects will also enjoy the photographic process more too, since an oblique angle lessens the chances of them being temporarily blinded by flashes.

3. A modest suggestion. Try not to take photographs when it is pitch black. Even without red-eye, they never seem to come out well anyway. Leave the cave photographs to the pros.

And why do cats and dogs seem to be especially prone to contracting red-eye in photographs? Both cats and dogs have larger and more open pupils than humans, which allow the flash to penetrate into their innocent retinas.

Submitted by Abby Mason of Canton, Ohio. Thanks also to Gene Newman of Broomall, Pennsylvania; Elanor Lynn of Worcester, Vermont; and Megan A. Martin of Chino, California.

Why Do Dogs Have Wet Noses?

To tell you the truth, we committed to this Imponderable as the title of the book before we had a definitive answer to it. When the deadline for the title faced us, we called some friends, Tom and Leslie Rugg, who have a large reference library about dogs, and asked them if there was any information in their books about dogs and wet noses. "Sure," they replied. They found several books that talked about sweat glands in dogs' noses that secrete fluid. The moisture of the nose evaporates as air is exhaled from the nostril, thus cooling off the dog.

Sounded good to us. Our title Imponderable was answerable.

An ethical dilemma nagged at us, though. We always claim that Imponderables are questions you can't easily find an answer to in books. And we like to find experts to answer our mysteries. Were we really going to allow our title Imponderable to be answered by other books? So we decided to confirm the answers supplied by the Ruggs' books.

Now we know where the phrase "Let sleeping dogs lie" comes from. The next month involved calls to numerous veterinarians, dog anatomists, zoologists, canine histologists, and even canine respiratory specialists. Without exception, they were gracious, knowledgeable, and interesting. But we have one serious complaint about dog experts, and scientists in general. They refuse to B.S.

How we long for the experts in the humanities and the social sciences, who have theories about everything and never let a lack of evidence get in the way of their pronouncements. But the most eminent dog researchers in the country, from prestigious veterinary schools like Cornell University and Iowa State University, insisted that we are closer to cloning human beings than we are to having a definitive answer to this Imponderable.

Here's what we do know. Most healthy dogs have wet noses most of the time. If a dog has a dry nose, it might just mean it has slept in a heated room, or buried its nose between its paws for an extended period. But it might also mean that the dog is dehydrated, often an early warning sign of illness. What causes the wetness in the first place? We heard three main theories:

1. The lateral nasal glands in a dog's nose secrete a fluid. Some of these glands are near the opening of the nostril and may be responsible for most of the moisture, but no one has proven how these secretions get to the tip of a dog's nose (there are no glands on the exterior of the nose).

2. Dr. Howard Evans of Cornell University believes that the wetness is probably a combination of secretions of the lateral nasal glands and the (nasal) vestibular glands.

3. Dr. Don Adams, a specialist in the respiratory system of canines at Iowa State University, adds that dogs often lick their noses with their tongues. Much of what we

perceive to be secretions on a dog's nose might actually be saliva.

So what function might a wet nose serve? Several theories here, too:

1. Most likely, the secretions of the nasal glands help the dog dissipate heat. Dogs do not sweat the way humans do. They dissipate most of their heat by panting with their tongues hanging out, evaporating from the moist surface of the tongue. While they pant, most of the air enters through their nose, which is more efficient than the mouth in evaporating water vapor. In his book *How Animals Work*, zoologist Knut Schmidt-Nielsen reports that

> in the dogs we tested, on the average about a quarter of the air inhaled through the nose was exhaled again through the nose, the remaining three-quarters being exhaled through the mouth. The amounts could vary a great deal, however, and at any given moment from zero to 100% of the inhaled air volume could be exhaled through the nose.

Schmidt-Nielsen's study indicated that exhaling through the mouth doubled dogs' heat loss, but when they were only slightly overheated, some dogs didn't pant at all. Schmidt-Nielsen indicated that the sole function of the nasal glands might be to provide moisture for heat exchange.

2. Lateral nasal glands contain odorant-binding particles that help dogs smell. Dr. Dieter Dellman of Cornell University told us that all animals can smell better when odors are picked up from a moist surface. Whether or not moisture on the *exterior* of a dog's nose actually aids in olfactory functions is not well established.

3. Dr. Adams thinks it is possible that the lateral nasal glands might be connected with salivary functions. He told us about a personal experience. Adams was measuring lat-

eral nasal gland secretions one day (we thought we had a weird job!) and felt sorry for the poor dog stuck wearing an Elizabethan collar. Secretions were coming in a steady trickle, until Adams decided to reward the dog with a few pieces of sausage. All of a sudden, the lateral nasal glands sprung a leak. Adams doesn't claim to understand what the connection is yet, but such accidental discoveries explain why scientists aren't apt to spout off about definitive answers until they can prove the veracity of the theory.

4. The wetness is a cosmic joke meant only to spoil the life of anyone who writes about it. This, of course, is our theory.

So, dear readers. If you should see us on television or speaking on the radio, promoting this book, and the host asks this Imponderable, please be advised that though our answer might be short and glib and we appear to be carefree, don't let our glad expression give you the wrong impression. We are really shedding the tears of a clown.

Every time we provide the simple, ten-second sound bite that the host craves but that doesn't really answer this Imponderable with the complexity it deserves, we are being paid back for premature title selection.

Submitted by Kelly Marrapodi of Tucson, Arizona. Thanks also to Erin Johnson of Marietta, Georgia, and Mike Surinak of Tucson, Arizona.

Why Don't You Ever See a Used UPS Truck?

Our correspondent, Robert A. Waldo, notes that driving about, one often sees second-owner trucks that betray the identity of their original owners. Perhaps a "U-HAUL," "FRITO-LAY," or "RYDER" will peek through a new paint job.

UPS maintains three kinds of vehicles in its fleet of over 100,000: vans; tractor-trailers; and its familiar brown delivery trucks, which UPS itself calls "package cars." The trucks are manufactured to UPS' specifications by General Motors, Ford, and Navistar. Although the chassis may differ, the bodies of the trucks are identical. The "package cars" are scrupulously maintained and washed at least once every other day. The lifespan of a package car is astonishingly high—between twenty and twenty-five years.

The secret to the disappearing UPS truck is simple. According to Serena Marks, a public relations representative of the United Parcel System, "Because of our high safety standards, once a package car has been taken permanently out of service it is destroyed." Maybe if the automobiles and trucks we bought for ourselves lasted twenty-five years, we could afford to destroy them rather than trading them in.

Submitted by Robert A. Waldo of Bothell, Washington.

THE CLEAVER MEMORIAL WARD

QUIET

GUARDED

STABLE

GRAVE

What Are the Guidelines for Stating That a Hospital Patient Is in "Good" or "Critical" Condition? Are the Standards Uniform among Hospitals?

Much to our surprise, there aren't uniform standards. We contacted many hospitals' public relations departments and found that they were much more preoccupied with protecting the privacy rights of patients than they were with pinpointing their condition. All of the hospitals directed me to the American Hospital Association, which issues a brochure written by Mary Laing Babich called "General Guide for the Release of Patient Information by the Hospital," which is adapted from a chapter of *Hospitals and the News Media: A Guide to Good Media Relations.*

Babich's guide includes two conditions used to describe patients whose vital signs are stable and within normal limits, "good" and "fair." The patient in good condition is comfortable and the indicators are excellent. The "fair" patient may be uncomfortable, but the indicators are favorable. Many hospitals use "stable" or "satisfactory" as a synonym for "fair."

A patient in "serious" condition "may be unstable and not within normal limits." This patient is acutely ill but not necessarily in imminent danger. The prognosis for the "serious" patient is unclear.

The "critical" patient always has unstable and abnormal vital signs and may be unconscious. The indicators are unfavorable.

"Unconscious" and "dead" are the other two conditions listed. The former is used when a patient is brought into the hospital in this condition before the prognosis or vital signs of the patient are established. Everyone knows what "dead" means, but releasing this information can be a difficult problem. According to Babich's guidelines, the death of a patient is a matter of public record but the hospital has the obligation to notify the next of kin first: "Information regarding the cause of death must come from the patient's physician, and its release must be approved by a member of the immediate family (when available)."

Despite the proliferation of the American Hospital Association's guidelines, we've noticed that hospital spokespersons often improvise their own terms at press conferences. "Very critical" and "grave" have been offered, probably as gingerly attempts to answer the unstated question that reporters really want to know: "When is this famous patient going to die?"

Submitted by Glenn Worthman of Palo Alto, California.

Why Is a Watch Called a "Watch"? After All, Do You Have to Watch a Watch Any More than You Have to Watch a Clock?

Huh?

Let's see who's on first here. First we go to our trusty dictionaries, which inform us that the word "watch" has the same Old English etymology as the words "wake" and "awaken." Were the first watches alarm clocks? Probably not. Some word historians have speculated that the word derives from an Old English word meaning "to keep vigil" and that the naming of the timepiece had to do with the fact that they were carried by night watchmen.

But the most fascinating, if unverifiable, etymology was provided by Stuart Berg Flexner in his book *Listening to America*. When watches were introduced, clocks had no hour or minute hands. Rather, clocks struck on the hour—a totally auditory signal (indeed, "clock" derives from the Latin word *cloca*, meaning "bell"). But watches sported minute and hour hands. One had to literally watch the watch to find out what time it was.

Submitted by Corporal Dorwin C. Shelton of Tarawa Terrace, North Carolina.

What's the Distinction between a Clock and a Watch?

The difference isn't merely size. Some old pocket watches were bigger than our travel clocks of today. Clocks were invented in Italy in the fourteenth century and watches followed more than a century later.

From the beginning, clocks were weight driven. But the breakthrough that made watches possible was the invention of a different technology to drive the device—the mainspring made of coiled steel.

Now that both clocks and watches use new technologies, the distinction between the two often hinges on size, portability, and where the timepiece is displayed.

Submitted by Cuesta Schmidt of West New York, New Jersey.

WHY DO DOGS HAVE WET NOSES?

How Did the Football Get Its Strange Shape?

If it weren't for the forces of civility, we might call the game "*head*ball" instead of football. For the earliest antecedent of football used human skulls as the ball.

The Danes occupied England in the early eleventh century. Shortly after the Danes were vanquished in 1042, an Englishman unearthed the skull of a buried Danish soldier and kicked it around his field. Others dug up Danish "headballs" and enjoyed the pastime of kicking them around but found the solidity of the object rather hard on the foot. So they looked for alternative sporting equipment. And they quickly found the obvious choice.

Inflated cow bladders, of course.

The game caught on and assumed the proportions of a mass psychosis. A bladder was dropped between two neighboring towns. If one team managed to kick the bladder into the center of the other's town, it won. Although contestants never touched the ball with their hands (indeed, they called the game futballe), they had no such compunctions about using their fists to hit each other.

King Henry II (1154–1189) banned the sport, not only to eliminate rampant vandalism and violence but because it posed a security threat. His soldiers were playing futballe instead of practicing their archery. For the next four hundred years, futballe was outlawed but continued to be played anyway.

The ban against futballe was lifted by James I (1603–1625), who bowed to the wishes of sportsmen. The game was legitimized by placing it in standardized playing fields and awarding points for passing the other team's goal. Cow bladders yielded to round balls. This game became known as Association Football. The shortening of the Association to Assoc. provided the slang expression "soccer," which is the sport's modern name.

The next historical development crucial to the history of American football occurred when a frustrated William Ellis, a college student in England, decided to pick up the soccer ball during a game and run with it. He scored the first illegal touchdown in 1823. Although at the time his behavior was not rewarded, his college is best known for his unsportsmanlike behavior. The name of his college: Rugby. (And now you know why this is the only sport whose name is often capitalized, at least when referring to English Rugby.)

Many early settlers in America played soccer, but the game caught on in the mid-nineteenth century among Ivy League colleges. Bob Carroll, of the Professional Football Researchers Association, sent us an entertaining account of how the shape of the American football evolved:

> The football got its shape before it was a football. The first intercollegiate game between Rutgers and Princeton in 1869 was no more football than roller derby is a steeplechase. They played soccer—and used a round soccer ball. When the college boys got to writing some rules in 1873, they specified that a "No. 6 ball" should be used.

WHY DO DOGS HAVE WET NOSES?

However, there were two No. 6 balls—a round one for soccer and one a bit more oblong for rugby. The reason these two different balls had evolved in England was that soccer, which depended upon kicking and "puddling" the ball along the ground, could only be played with a round (or "puddle-able") ball. In Rugby, though, a player could run with the ball before he kicked it. Well, it don't take a whole lot of smarts to figure out you can hold onto a fat, prolate spheroid easier than a fat sphere. Think of the fumbles if we played football with a basketball!

In 1874, the boys from McGill University in Canada taught the soccer players from Harvard how to play Rugby. Then Harvard taught Princeton, Yale and Columbia. In the early 1880s, Walter Camp pushed through rules that changed American rugby to American football. By 1883, touchdowns counted more than kicked goals, which meant the ball was soon tapered even more to make it even easier to run with.

The forward pass was legalized in 1906 and by 1913 became a fairly common occurrence [the emergence of the forward pass can be traced to a 1913 Notre Dame game against Army when Gus Dorais and the legendary Knute Rockne combined to pass for a dramatic victory]. That led, over a period of time, to more thinning of the ball so it could be passed and make those pretty spirals we all know and love. The more passing—the skinnier the football. If they keep changing rules to help the passers, by 2025, football will be played with a javelin.

Submitted by William Marschall of Edenton, North Carolina. Thanks also to Mike Pintek, KDKA, Pittsburgh, Pennsylvania; Jena Mori of Los Angeles, California; Fred White of Mission Viejo, California; and Patrick M. Premo of Allegany, New York.

HERE'S MY RING! I KNEW WE'D GET IT OUT WITH THE SNAKE!

Why Is the Piping under Kitchen Sinks So Circuitous? Why Is It "S"-Shaped? Why Not Just Have One Straight Vertical Pipe?

Believe us, Colleen, this is not a plot by the plumbing industry to sell you more piping. You want those curves.

The piping under sinks (and under lavatories, for that matter) is called a "P" trap. The curvy pipe dips down below the horizontal pipe so that a water seal is formed in the bend, assuring that water, and not air, will fill the area below the horizontal pipe.

Why would you want to create a deliberate water blockage? Because the water blocks sewer and other foul smells from drifting up the pipe and into the room.

And on occasion, the "P" trap blocks certain items from going downstream. Gary Felsinger, a marketing manager at Kohler Co., explains: "In some cases, the "P" trap also saves valuable rings from falling into the sewer when accidentally dropped down the drain."

Submitted by Colleen Uehara of San Jose, California.

What Is the Meaning of the Codes on Colored Stickers Affixed to Some Envelopes by the Post Office?

After the mail has been sorted at the post office, the mail is bundled according to its destination. The postal worker grabs a handful of mail and fastens it with a rubber band lengthwise and another rubber band widthwise. On the top of each bundle, he or she affixes a sticker that designates the following code:

> "F" on a blue sticker stands for "firm." The whole bundle is addressed to one company.
>
> "D" on a red sticker stands for "direct." All of the mail in that bundle is headed for one particular five-digit ZIP code.
>
> "C" on a yellow sticker stands for "city." The mail is going to one city, and the first three digits are the same on each piece (e.g., all ZIP codes in Kansas City start with 641).
>
> "3" on a green sticker stands for "3-digit area." Not all cities are large enough to claim exclusive rights to all three of the first ZIP code digits. "3" bundles are going to a Sectional Center Facility that might route the mail to several different towns or cities that share the same first three digits.
>
> "A" on a pink sticker stands for "Area Distribution Center." Some cities have more than one three-digit ZIP code. The "A" is an attempt to send the bundle to the distribution center closest to where the mail is actually being delivered, even if it doesn't qualify for a "C" sticker.

We asked Karen E. McAliley, of the Consumer Affairs Department of the United States Postal Service, how postal workers decide which envelopes to place the stickers on. McAliley replied that it is the luck of the draw. Whichever envelope happens to be on top of the bundle receives the honor. The bundles are then hand-tossed into appropriate sacks and go their way.

Submitted by Dan Proper of Chapin, South Carolina.

WHY DO DOGS HAVE WET NOSES?

Why Don't Food Manufacturers Put Their Street Address on Their Labels?

Because they don't have to. Why encourage crackpot letters? Why waste space on the label with a street address when you can increase the size of the words "New and Improved" on the label by one-eighth of an inch?

But manufacturers are required by the federal government to list their name, the city, state, and ZIP code of their company. They must put their street address on the label only if their place of business is not listed in a telephone or city directory. So if you want to write that nasty letter, and the street address isn't printed on the label, directory assistance can always locate the company for you.

Submitted by Carl Allen of Los Angeles, California.

AND OTHER IMPONDERABLES

At Weddings, Why Do We Congratulate the Groom and Wish the Bride Happiness? Is It Considered to Be Unlucky or Simply Poor Manners to Congratulate the Bride?

In our experience, the tradition makes sense. The groom deserves congratulations and the bride needs all the luck she can muster.

Several etiquette books we consulted continue to recommend the practice, even though it is rooted in the basest form of sexism. Jaclyn C. Barrett, of *Southern Bride,* told us that "Congratulations!" to the bride somehow is interpreted as "I can't believe you actually landed a man!" Still, all of our sources indicated that it wasn't considered unlucky to extend congratulations to the bride—just poor form.

Congratulating the groom, according to *Bride*'s associate editor Melanie Martini, stems from the ancient notion of marriage as the capture of a woman by a man. Saying "Congratulations!" to the groom is translated as "Nice trout!"

Submitted by Barrie Creedon of Philadelphia, Pennsylvania.

Why Are All Gondolas Black?

This Imponderable was thrown at us on Jim Eason's KGO talk show in San Francisco. We were totally stumped but many subsequent callers offered their theories, most having to do with the advantage of black in absorbing the sun. We were skeptical, since not too many boats we have ever seen were painted black.

We considered flying out to Venice to check out this Imponderable personally (a legitimate research expense, no?), but unfortunately we stumbled upon the answer before we obtained our passport.

The origins of these boats are obscure; no one can find the derivation of the word "gondola." Gondolas have probably existed since the eleventh century and probably were painted many different colors. But in 1562, a sumptuary law was passed in Venice mandating that all gondolas be painted black. Many sumptuary laws were primarily attempts to avoid extravagant or unnecessary expenditures. But during this period, the Catholic church encouraged the passage of laws that banned ostentation for its own sake, particularly in matters of dress and decoration.

Still, the Italian flash has always shone through in the gondola. For in contrast to its somber color, the gondola sports a gleaming ferro that decorates the upcurving prow of the boat. Nobody knows whether the seven metal prongs on the prow ever had a symbolic meaning or if they were purely ornamental, but the steel ferro has always undermined the intention of the sumptuary law.

Why Do Many Soft Drink Labels Say "5 Mg. or Less Sodium per 6 oz. Serving" When the Labels Also Claim the Drink Is "Sodium-free"?

As if to prove he wasn't crazy, Douglas Watkins sent us a Schweppes label with both of the claims stated above. With its usual gift of the mother tongue, the American government (specifically, the Food and Drug Administration) has declared that "sodium-free" doesn't really mean the drink contains no sodium but rather five milligrams or fewer per serving. Serving sizes can vary, but most soft drink companies use 6 ounces as the standard.

Even more obviously subjective terms have exacting sodium requirements. "Very low sodium" drinks contain 35 milligrams or less sodium per serving; "low sodium" drinks have 140 milligrams or fewer.

"Reduced sodium" claims must be backed up with proof

that the drink has reduced the original amount of sodium by at least 75 percent. "No salt added," "unsalted," and "without added salt" are all official terms that signify that no salt is added during processing when salt normally is used.

As much as it pains us to be fair to a bureaucracy, we must admit that it would probably be counterproductive for the FDA to insist that "sodium free" means absolutely no sodium. Many foods have trace amounts of sodium that pose no danger to people on even the most restrictive diets. Do we really need labels that proclaim "minuscule sodium"?

Submitted by Douglas Watkins, Jr. of Hayward, California.

WHY DO DOGS HAVE WET NOSES?

now you can

Bake up
crunchier
Muffins!

Baker's
surprise
Flour
with
SPONTANEOUS
GENERATION

Protein-
enriched!

Why Do Bugs Seem to Suddenly Appear in Flour, Cornmeal, and Fruit? Where Do They Come From?

If you want to disabuse yourself of the notion that your house or apartment is a haven, a calm and clean refuge from the chaos of the outside world, consult David Bodanis' *The Secret House,* a study of the natural world inside our houses. With the help of scary, graphic photographs, Bodanis shows us that for every cockroach we might see scampering across our kitchen floor at night, there are thousands of bed mites, microscopic insects that subsist largely on a balanced diet of shedded human skin and hair.

Any time you slam a newspaper down on the dining room table or spray deodorant in the bathroom, you are traumatizing thousands of little critters. So it shouldn't be too surprising that the insects in our houses become interested in other types of food. Raw, unbleached flour may not be too appetizing to us, but compared to hair droppings, it becomes a reasonable alternative.

AND OTHER IMPONDERABLES

Many insects infest food before it is packaged, often in the form of eggs. According to Dr. George W. Rambo, of the National Pest Control Association, these insects are called "stored product insects." Everyone in the food industry expects a few insects and/or rodent hairs to infest many kinds of food; the Food and Drug Administration acknowledges the inevitability by mandating maximum limits.

Even if insects are not in the flour or fruit when you purchase it, they are attracted to the food once you bring it home. Flour might seem bland to you, but to grain mites or meal worms, it smells like ambrosia.

Many of the insects that infest flour, for example, are barely visible to the eye. It's a snap for a bug less than one-eighth of an inch long to intrude into packaging, especially after it has been opened.

So it's a losing fight. Our advice is to worry about the ones you can see and try not to think about the others.

Submitted by Karole Rathouz of Mehlville, Missouri. Thanks also to Jill Palmer of Leverett, Massachusetts; Scott Parker of Beaumont, Texas; Nicole Locke of Belmont, Massachusetts; Jane Doty of Tigard, Oregon; and Beverly Ditolla of Arvada, California.

Why Are the Large Staples Used to Fasten Cardboard Cartons Made of Expensive Copper?

They aren't. Carton staples are made out of steel wire. But they are finished with a very thin coating of a copper-sulfate solution, which gives the staples the appearance of copper. According to John Nasiatka, an engineer at the Duo-Fast Corporation, this is known as a "liquor" finish. Scrape a staple with a knife, and you will see how thin the coating is.

The copper-sulfate coating is not applied for aesthetic reasons; it provides real, if limited, rust protection.

One company we contacted, Redmore Products, reports that it makes staples from wire with a heavy copper coating. These staples are designed for electric utilities. The extra copper provides a longer life and helps prevent electrolysis (and we're not talking about hair removal).

Submitted by Clifford Abrams of Evanston, Illinois.

Why Does *TV Guide* Start Its Listings on Saturday?

When *TV Guide* first began in 1953, Saturday was one of the nights that attracted the greatest number of television viewers. Such blockbuster shows as "The Jackie Gleason Show," "The Original Amateur Hour," "Your Show of Shows," and "Your Hit Parade" all appeared on Saturday.

Sunday was then an even bigger night, but sales of *TV Guide* weren't high on Sundays. Many cities had strict blue laws that forbade stores, including supermarkets, from conducting business on Sundays. *TV Guide* feared that consumers who couldn't buy the magazine on Sunday might forgo the purchase altogether. By listing programs starting with Saturday, *TV Guide* could attract working couples doing their grocery shopping on Friday night or Saturday.

Patrick Murphy, programming editor of *TV Guide*, told *Imponderables* that the original decision was made entirely by the editorial department, but now there are production reasons for keeping the listings starting on Saturday. Saturday is the networks' biggest sports day. Last-minute schedule changes are often made in line-ups for football and basketball games. By starting with Saturday, *TV Guide* can wait until the "last minute" to commit to printing which teams will be playing. And now that Saturday is one of the nights that draws the fewest viewers, shoppers who don't buy the magazine on Saturday might still buy it on Sunday (the night with the most sets in use), now that blue laws are a thing of the past.

Submitted by David Wedryk of South Holland, Illinois. Thanks also to David A. Kroffe of Los Alamitos, California.

IS There any Difference between a "NO OUTLET" and a "DEAD-END" Sign?

Not much. According to the *Manual on Uniform Traffic Control Devices*, there is no technical distinction between the two signs. But Harry Skinner, chief, Traffic Engineering Division of the Office of Traffic Operations at the Federal Highway Administration, says that there is a subtle difference in practice:

> the DEAD END sign will commonly be used for roads or streets that terminate within sight of the driver whereas a NO OUTLET is more often used to sign a road or street which is the only entrance and exit to a neighborhood.

Submitted by Donna M. Auguste of Menlo Park, California.

Why Do Ironworkers Wear Their Hard Hats Backwards?

Unless an inordinate number of ironworkers were absentminded baseball catchers on the side, we had no explanation for this Imponderable until we heard from James B. Ford, of Local 396 in St. Louis, and editor of *Journeyman Ironworker*.

Ford, an ironworker with 25 years' experience, swatted away the Imponderable with ease:

> . . . the majority of the time, we are wearing welding goggles on the job. By wearing our hard hat backwards, it enables us to pull the goggles up onto our foreheads without removing the hard hat each time. Of course, we wear hard hats for safety reasons; so at the same time we are observing the safety rules, we have the convenience of easy goggle removal.

Submitted by Frank Overstreet of Fred, Texas.

Why Is Red Wine Supposed to Be Served at Room Temperature and White Wine Chilled?

A recent article in the *New York Times* reported that despite expectations of a boom, wine sales had flattened in the United States during the 1980s. Although affluent Americans started buying much more wine in the 1970s, the industry's attempts to seduce average Americans with anything other than wine coolers obviously failed in the 1980s.

What happened? Although the average person might reply that he doesn't want to spend $6.00 for a bottle of wine in a liquor store, or $20.00 for the identical bottle at a restaurant, the same guy will spend $1.50 for a bottle of Evian water that tastes remarkably like tap water.

We think there is another possibility. The average person is afraid of wine and the whole rigamarole surrounding it. Who wants to take a special date out to a nice restaurant and proceed to mispronounce the name of the wine and then get a chilly look from the waiter when he orders *that* wine ("Was that red wine with fish?" the poor shlub wonders. "Or white wine with fish? And what do I do if I get a steak and she orders fish—order pink wine? Come to think of it, there is a pink wine—isn't there?"). And then, worst of all, our poor shlub has to pretend he knows what he is doing when the waiter or wine steward pours the wine in his glass for inspection. He knows that the waiter knows that he doesn't have the slightest idea how to even pretend that he is actually judging the quality of the wine rather than merely attempting to avoid looking like a bumbling idiot.

All this and then you have to pay through the nose for the privilege of being humiliated. Personally speaking, we'd still rather order wine out in a restaurant than at home. We have a remarkably poor record of extracting the cork intact. When more wine comes with screw-tops, we'll consider becoming enologists.

One of the great truths handed down to us from Mount Olympus is that it is a cardinal sin to chill red wine. We've read this rule scores of times but without an explanation. We are happy to announce that we found some wine experts who could explain the practice and clear away some of the mystique. We yield the floor to Sam Folsom, of San Francisco's Wine Institute:

> Red wine contains a number of natural acids, most notably tannin [tannic acid], and other components that aren't found in white wine. This is because red wines are fermented with the grape skins, while white wines are not. Many of these natural acids are found in the skin of the grape.
>
> When red wine is chilled, these natural acids are exacerbated, while the grape flavors are masked. This results in a wine that tastes harsh without any other flavor components. At room temperature, the natural acids are much more in balance with the grape flavors, making the wine much more appealing. White wines are refreshing chilled and don't suffer the same flavor imbalances when chilled because they do not contain tannin and other acids.

We spoke to Barbara Mader Ivey, national director of Women on Wine, a woman who proves that it is possible to be an expert on

WHY DO DOGS HAVE WET NOSES?

wine and have a sense of humor at the same time. She confirms that most red wines taste best at room temperature but suggests common sense. If your room happens to be a nonairconditioned one in Palm Springs during the summer, a sweetish nouveau beaujolais will not be at its best at "room temperature." And although chilling enhances most white wines, she suggests that good wine will have a fine flavor at any room temperature; if anything, most people err on the side of overchilling white wine.

Submitted by Roy Welland of New York, New York. Thanks also to Charles Myers of Ronkonkoma, New York.

Why, After a Call on a Pay Phone, Does One Hear a Click That Sounds Like the Money is Coming Back Down to the Refund Slot?

We dare say that if we plumbed deep into our souls, we would admit that we have, on more than one occasion, heard the unmistakable sound of coins dropping after completing a call and checked the refund slot to make sure our quarter hadn't come back. Of course, we fully intended to reinsert the quarter. We just wanted to make sure that our quarter didn't fall into the wrong hands and thereby shortchange the phone company. Right?

The sound you hear after hanging up the phone is indeed the sound of your coin(s) falling down. Shelly Gilbreath, of Southwestern Bell Telephone, explains:

> When the call is complete, and the customer at the coin phone hangs up, or the call times out, an audible "click" is heard. This "click" is the sound that the coin phone equipment recognizes as a signal to allow the money to drop from the reservoir into a small metal compartment inside the coin phone. There are employees within the phone companies that come around and unlock the front of the coin phone [we answered the mystery of why you

never see these employees in *Imponderables*], and collect the coins that are in the compartment.

Submitted by Todd Nickerson of Londonderry, New Hampshire.

Why Do So Few Houses in the South Have Basements?

Weather. Architect Bill Stanley told *Imponderables* that many southern communities have high water tables that can flood basements. In wet areas, some houses are built on stilts to forestall the potential problem.

But basements are more practical in colder climates and don't cost that much extra to build. Dennis McClendon, managing editor of the American Planning Association's *Planning* magazine, and a transplanted southerner, explains why:

> Southern homebuilders don't have to go very far below ground to place the house's foundation below the frost line. To avoid heaving and cracking, a house's foundation must go below the frost line (the depth to which the ground can be expected to freeze).
>
> Building codes in the North typically require foundations several feet below ground level. Since the builder has already had to excavate that deep for foundations, it makes sense to treat the foundations as walls and finish the space inside as a basement. It also makes connection to water and sewer lines (which must be below the frost line) easier. Tradition also plays a part: Home buyers who are used to the space a basement provides expect one in a new home.

Submitted by Jon R. Kennedy of Charlotte, North Carolina.

WHY DO DOGS HAVE WET NOSES?

Why Is Sugar an Ingredient in Most Commercially Packaged Salt?

It is? So we wondered when we received Stephanie Drossin's Imponderable. We went to our cupboard and found our container of Morton's salt.

Waddya know? Dextrose is listed as an ingredient. We immediately dispatched a letter to Morton International and received an enlightening response from advertising/sales promotion supervisor Kathleen M. Reidy:

> Dextrose is added to Morton Iodized Table Salt in order to ensure optimum salt flavor characteristics and to stabilize the iodide. Iodide is added as it is vital to the proper function of the thyroid gland and in the prevention of goiter.
>
> Actually, the amount of dextrose in salt is so small that it is dietetically insignificant. Morton Iodized Table Salt contains 0.04 percent dextrose or 40 milligrams per 100 grams of salt.
>
> For many years dextrose was also added to Morton Plain Table Salt. However, dextrose was removed from Morton Plain Table Salt in 1980 to allay the fears of those concerned with their sugar intake.

We don't know about iodide stabilization, but we will confirm that adding sugar to just about anything ensures optimum flavor. Whenever we're cooking and faced with a dish that just doesn't work, sugar seems like a mystical cureall.

But now that we've made both sodium and sugar out to be nutritional bad guys, and now that we've let the cat out of the bag about sugar in salt, we're anticipating the launching of a new product, Diet Salt. That's right. Salt with artificial sweetener.

Sure, salt isn't fattening. But by saving those milligrams of sugar over ten years, you will have saved enough calories to indulge yourself in a whole Hershey's Kiss.

Submitted by Stephanie Drossin of Philadelphia, Pennsylvania.

Is It True That Women Who Live Together Tend to Synchronize Their Menstrual Cycles? If So, Why Does This Happen?

Yes, it's true. In a 1971 article in *Nature,* M. K. McClintock provided hard research to confirm what women had long claimed: Women who live together tend to have synchronous cycles. Subsequent researchers have corroborated McClintock's findings. Nobody can explain the phenomenon yet, but many possible explanations have been eliminated.

The American College of Obstetricians and Gynecologists led us to a 1989 article in the *American Journal of Human Biology* that confronts this Imponderable head-on. Written by three medical doctors (B. B. Little, D. S. Guzick, and R. M. Malina) and one anthropologist (M. D. Rocha Ferreira), "Environmental Influences Cause Menstrual Synchrony, Not Pheromones" reports the findings of a fascinating research experiment.

They studied 127 female college students who lived in a group of 12 houses that surrounded a common courtyard. The study was conducted in the fall and none of the women had lived together during the summer.

The conclusions were startling. During the first month of coresidence, the day of menstrual onset deviated from the mean by an average of 13.7 days. During the next month, the average deviation declined to 2.6 days! Although a high degree of synchrony was achieved in one month of coresidence, the second month added only 0.3 day increase in synchrony.

By collecting all kinds of demographic and personal information, the researchers were able to rule out any other obvious correlations. They found no statistical correlation, for example, between synchrony and age, exercise patterns, or years since menarche. Other studies have shown that mothers, daughters, and sisters do not tend to have a higher than expected number of synchronous menstrual periods unless they live together.

Previous investigators suggested that pheromonal influences might have caused synchrony. But one of this study's findings tends to dispute this theory: Living in the same house tended to slightly increase synchrony, but explained only a small part of the variance. If the pheromonal secretions were the key to menstrual cycles,

> roommates and coresidents should have been significantly synchronized and women who did not live together should not have been synchronized. In contrast, the results of this study indicate that a large component of the variation in menstrual cycling is environmental (i.e., shared variance), perhaps as much as 91%. Thus, coresidence may be a surrogate for common environmental effects on synchrony, and not necessarily an opportunity for exposure to pheromones.

The researchers of this study don't speculate on precisely what these environmental factors are. It wasn't diet, because each house planned its own menus, so college "mystery meat" isn't the answer. Perhaps the shared hours and routine (all the women had a midnight curfew and a ban on male visitors after hours) contributed. So although we don't yet know the etiology of synchronous cycles, at least, as Kassie Schwan's illustration suggests, we know that they can be conveniently efficient.

Submitted by Rocco Manzo of St. Louis, Missouri.

Why Are Blueprints Blue?

Not because architects wanted to dabble in primary colors. No one would disagree that white lines on blue paper aren't easy to read.

But the paper is cheap. The salts used in blueprint processing are what turns them blue when developed. Dennis McClendon, of the American Planning Association, told *Imponderables* that the silver salts used in photography yield a nice black tone that reads well against white paper. But silver salts are expensive and difficult to develop.

About one hundred years ago, original architectural drawings were done with pen and ink, a costly, labor-intensive process. So the technology of blueprinting was developed to reproduce originals relatively cheaply; blueprinting technology didn't change much for almost a century.

Blueprinting was a wet process in which the original pen and ink drawing was made on translucent tracing paper. The paper was put in contact with paper coated with a ferro (iron)-prussiate (salt) mixture. This coating turned the finished blueprint blue.

The blueprint was then exposed to ultraviolet light, developed in potash, rinsed in water, and dried. Originally, the prints were left out in the sun to dry, but later they were artificially exposed in blueprint machines using carbon arcs or mercury vapor lamps. The original pen and ink lines reproduced as white and the blank areas reproduced as solid blue.

The blueprinting process proved to be cheap, relatively fast, and reliable. Only one problem loomed: Nobody liked reading blueprints.

To the rescue came the diazo process. Diazo materials are coated not with iron and prussiate salts but with diazonium salts and a coupler (which eventually colors the print) that are developed in ammonia fumes. The biggest advantage of the diazo process is that after the drawing is exposed to ultraviolet light, the clear portions of the original are rendered white (or light) and the opaque markings appear dark (usually blue). One can read "whiteprints" without eyestrain.

By the late 1950s, the diazo process, which had been invented in the late 1920s, had largely displaced blueprinting as a favored means of reproducing architectural drawings. Many architects and most laymen still nostalgically refer to whiteprints as "blueprints."

Soon there may be nostalgia for whiteprints. For diazo reproduction is losing its market share to LDXCs (large document xerographic copiers). The machines themselves are very expensive, but most architectural firms love their convenience. If nothing else, LDXCs don't leave the reproduction room smelling like ammonia. Now that they have been turned into an anachronism, blueprints have a right to be blue.

Submitted by Herbert Kraut of Forest Hills, New York. Thanks also to Laurence Ince of Briarwood, New York.

How Can Babies Withstand Higher Body Temperatures Than Their Supposedly Hardier Parents?

When adults spring a high fever, they are likely to be very sick. But babies often spike to high temperatures without serious repercussions. Babies' temperatures respond more quickly, more easily, and with much greater swings than adults'.

Why? Our body has a thermostat, located in the hypothalamus of the brain. When we are infected by bacteria or a virus, toxins interfere with the workings of the thermostat, fooling it into thinking that 103 degrees Fahrenheit, not 98.6 degrees, is "normal." With a baby, a 103-degree fever doesn't necessarily mean a more severe illness than a 101-degree fever.

Babies simply do not possess the well-developed hypothalamus that adults do. Temperature stability and regulation, like other developmental faculties, steadily increase as the baby ages.

Fever is a symptom, not the cause of sickness. In fact, fever is both a bodily defense against infection and a reliable alarm.

The first reaction of most parents to their babies' fevers is to bundle them up like Eskimos, especially when taking them outside. Mother and father don't always know best. Fever isn't really the enemy and shouldn't be treated as such. The body is trying to fight infection by raising the temperature. Swaddling the baby actually interferes with the heat loss that will eventually ease the fever.

Submitted by Ron Pateman of Chicago, Illinois.

What Accounts for the Varying Amounts of Static Electricity from Day to Day? Why is There More Static Electricity in the Winter Than During the Summer?

With the help of Richard Anthes, president of the University Corporation for Atmospheric Research, we can lay out the answer to this Imponderable with a logical precision that Mr. Wizard would admire.

1. Static electricity relies upon the buildup of an electrical charge difference between two objects and the sudden release of this difference in an electrical spark.
2. In order to build up a charge difference sufficient to create static electricity, there should not be much electrical conductivity in the air.
3. The conductivity of moist air is greater than the conductivity of dry air.
4. Relative humidity inside houses or other buildings is usually much lower in the winter than the summer.
5. Therefore, static electricity is more likely to occur in the winter than in the summer.

Static electricity can occur in the summer if the humidity happens to be low that day or if air conditioning dehumidifies the air inside.

Submitted by Reverend Ken Vogler of Jeffersonville, Indiana.

Why Do We Kiss Under the Mistletoe?

The innocuous mistletoe plant, now used to cop a cheap kiss or two, was once considered to be a sacred plant by the ancient Druids. They believed that mistletoe could cure sicknesses and shield its owner from evil forces such as witches or ghosts. Druids gathered the plant at winter solstice, just days before we now celebrate Christmas. With great solemnity and ritual, they cut the mistletoe with a golden sickle reserved solely for this purpose.

So sacred was the mistletoe to the Druids that they never allowed the plant to touch the ground, which probably explains why we still hang mistletoe over our doorways. The Druids believed that by placing the mistletoe over their doorways, they could not only protect the health and safety of all who passed through but also promote romance and fertility. If a boy kissed a girl under the mistletoe and gave one of the plants's white berries to the kissee, the ritual meant they would get married within the year.

Ironically, although mistletoe is now associated with Christmas, the Christians in Celtic regions, ashamed of their pagan antecedents, did everything possible to dissociate themselves from the belief in the power of mistletoe. But the practice took hold. And although a buss under the mistletoe no longer promises marriage, at least we've retained the fun part of the ritual.

Submitted by Brian Hart of Bala Cynwyd, Pennsylvania. Thanks also to Jeffrey R. Reder of Mahopac, New York; Gail Lee of Los

Angeles, California; Karin Norris of Salinas, California; Nadine L. Sheppard of Fairfield, California; and Jena Mori of Los Angeles, California.

What Do the Numbers on Pasta Boxes Mean?

The biggest marketers of packaged pastas, such as Ronzoni, Prince, and Mueller's, make such a bewildering array of pastas that numbers were assigned to help consumers discriminate among the varieties. Unfortunately, each company has their own system, and the numbers are arbitrarily assigned.

Frank Taufiq, vice-president of quality assurance for the Prince Company, told *Imponderables* that his company makes more than 80 different shapes and sizes of pasta. All are given numbers, in the hope that it will be easier for the consumer to remember numbers 56 and 57 than that they signify mostaccioli and mostaccioli with lines, respectively.

We have seen shoppers with glazed expressions trying to find the pasta variety that they once enjoyed but cannot remember or even pronounce if they did remember. The numbering system would undoubtedly help more people find the right pasta if supermarkets arranged pasta on their shelves in numerical order.

We once found a supermarket that placed all of Campbell's soups in alphabetical order. We might not have bought more soup as a result, but we sure spent less time in the soup aisle.

Submitted by Tom and Marcia Bova of Rochester, New York.
Thanks also to Howard Givner of Brooklyn, New York.

How Do Worms Survive During the Winter? Can They Crawl and Find Food?

They do just fine, thank you. Richard Zack, curator/director of the James Entomological Collection in Washington, explains:

> Worms continue to live and crawl around during the winter, usually below the freeze level. Their activity does slow and they would appear relatively inactive as compared to the summer. Remember, in most of our country the ground rarely freezes to much of a depth and snow is actually a good insulator from freezing temperatures and winds. If a worm were to be caught in frozen ground it would remain inactive, but alive, until the ground thawed.

Submitted by Robert Commaille of Bethel, Connecticut.

Why Do Worms Come out on the Sidewalk After It Rains?

What's with this sudden obsession over worms? Are the nineties going to be the Decade of the Larva?

What do you think the worms are coming out for? Their health? In fact, they are. Except for those that live as parasites, most worms live by burrowing little holes in the ground. When it rains, those little holes fill with water. If the worms didn't get out of the holes, they'd drown. Worms may be creepers, but they're not dolts.

Why do they congregate on the sidewalk after a rain? Two reasons. Sidewalks provide more solid support than dirt or grass during a rainstorm. But if you read our discussion of why ants congregate on the sidewalk (in *Why Do Clocks Run Clockwise?*), you've probably guessed the other explanation. The sidewalk provides a nice white background for us to see dark objects, worms, and insects. But if you investigated the grass adjacent to the sidewalk, you would find many worms trying to stay above water, wishing they had made it to the sidewalk.

> *Submitted by Mike Arnett of Chicago, Illinois. Thanks also to Karole Rathouz of Mehlville, Missouri; John P. Eichman of Yucaipa, California; Willard Wheeler of Upland, California; and Tom Trauschke of Whitehall, Pennsylvania.*

Why Don't Place Settings Use Serrated Knives?

In *Imponderables,* we discussed how mean old Cardinal Richelieu decreed in the seventeenth century that all dinner knives must have rounded edges in order to eradicate the serious social problem of dinner guests picking their teeth with sharp-edged knives. Ever since, the western world has been stuck with knives up to the task of spreading butter but inappropriate for cutting meat.

Now that there isn't too much danger of folks using their knives as toothpicks, might we go back to the old days of pointed knives? Why must we have separate "steak knives" to perform the chore for which knives were originally intended? Even rounded, serrated knives would cut meat more easily than the typical dinner knife and would still be able to spread butter effectively.

The reason our wish is but a pipe dream comes from Robert M. Johnston, who represents the Sterling Silversmiths Guild of America:

> The serration in a knife aids in its cutting. The serration is also apt to damage fine china and therefore is seldom used on a place knife in silverware.

Submitted by Richard Aaron of Toronto, Ontario.

Is There Any Meaning to the Numbers in Men's Hat Sizes?

Yes. But please don't ask for the full story—it is very complicated.

The American hat size is based on a measurement of the circumference of the head. The average man's head is about 23 inches in circumference. Divide 23 by pi (3.1416) and you get a number resembling 7⅜, a common hat size. The English, French, and Italians all have their own systems, also based on the circumference of the head.

In practice, most American hat manufacturers determine their sizes by measuring the length of the sweat band inside the hat and dividing by pi.

Submitted by Herman E. London of Poughkeepsie, New York.

What Is the Purpose of the Small Hole in the Barrel of Cheap Stick Pens?

We were first asked this question by a caller on Tom Snyder's syndicated radio show. Tom Snyder, upon hearing the question, proceeded to laugh his patented Tom Snyder laugh (or is it his Dan Ackroyd laugh?) and we knew we had to find the answer.

Susan Thompson, of A. T. Cross, makers of noncheap pens, told us that the innocuous little hole is of vital importance to a stick pen. Without the hole, a vacuum would be created in the pen as the ink was used and the pen wouldn't write.

R. F. Rhode, physical laboratory supervisor for Sheaffer Pen, concurs that if no air were allowed to enter the assembly and the parts of the pen were airtight, the pen would not write. Rhode adds that the hole serves another important function: equalizing the atmospheric pressure inside and outside the pen. Without equalized pressure, sensitive ballpoint pens tend not to write and start leaking (for more on leaking, see below).

Submitted by Vince Tassinari of West Springfield, Virginia.

What Causes Ink "Hemorrhages" in Pens?

Remember all the way back to the last Imponderable, when we were rambling on about air pressure? Here's the payoff. Air pressure is usually the culprit in the leaks of aqueous fountain pens. Sheaffer Pen's R. F. Rhode explains:

> If the pen is only partially filled with ink, there is considerable air in the sac or cartridge that holds the main ink supply. If there is a pressure change caused by a temperature change or an altitude change, and the pen is held point down or horizontal, the air expands and the pressure caused by this forces the thin aqueous ink out of the feeding system onto paper, clothing, etc.

O.K. Maybe the folks featured on *Lifestyles of the Rich and Famous* use fountain pens and jet to Aspen and have to suffer through the agonies of altitude adjustment. But why do the cheap pens that most of us use leak all the time?

Once when we were teaching, we bought a ten-pack of guaranteed student-torture devices, red pens. All ten of these beauties hemorrhaged within a few weeks. Infuriated, we sent eight of the leaky corpses back to the manufacturer, demanding a refund. We got back a curious note, along with ten fresh replacements, acknowledging the defects but saying in effect, "What do you expect from cheap pens? If you want a pen that doesn't leak, buy a good pen."

A malfunctioning ballpoint is the most likely cause of a stick pen's hemorrhage. Why do ballpoints malfunction? Common reasons include: manufacturing defects; excessive pressure by the user; dropping the pen; and temperature shifts. Pilot Corporation's Mimi Clark adds that leaking can also occur if the ink is too viscous and/or the size of the point is not sufficient to accommodate the ink flow coming down the barrel.

Ballpoint refills also have leaky tendencies. R. F. Rhode explains why:

> Usually this occurs on the larger diameter ballpoint refills that contain a follower-type material on top of the ink column. If there is a "break" in this follower-type material, ink will leak out the back end of ballpoint refills. Another cause can be excessive accumulation of ink around the ball in the tip—this is known as "leaking" or "gooping."

"Gooping" may be slang, but when the ink that is supposed to be in your pen is all over your hands and papers, no word is more descriptive.

Submitted by Gerald P. Cuccio of Downsview, Ontario.

Why Don't Women's Blouses Come in Sleeve Lengths, Like Men's Shirts?

Because there is no standard sleeve length for women's blouses. Cory Greenspan, of the Federation of Apparel Manufacturers, explains that the "appropriate" length of a woman's sleeve varies depending upon the dictates of the fashion designer and the purpose of the outfit. Men's long-sleeve shirts are designed to be worn with a jacket so that the sleeve will hang just below the wrist line when the wearer is standing. But women wear long-sleeve blouses with other garments or no covering at all.

Women have a much wider choice of blouses than men do of dress shirts. If each blouse came with sleeve sizes, retailers would have to cut down on their selection in order to provide all the different sizes. While men are content with the usual boring solids and stripes, even the dressiest of women's blouses are available in a wide range of colors and textures.

For the same inventory reasons, most men's shirts are now sold with "average" sleeve lengths. While the neck size is specified (e.g., 16), the "average" sleeve length may be 32/33. We expected to hear that the actual sleeve length of a 32/33 shirt is 32½ inches. But Mark Weber, of Phillips-Van Heusen, told *Imponderables* that the actual length is always the higher of the two numbers (in this case, 33 inches). By using "average" sleeve lengths, retailers can cut the number of different sizes of the same style shirt in half and use the saved space to display a greater variety of styles.

Submitted by Melanie Jongsma of Lansing, Illinois. Thanks also to Robert A. McKnight of Jennings, Missouri.

Why Are the American Quart and Gallon Smaller than the British Imperial Equivalents?

The American colonists adopted most of the weights and measures of Old England, including the British system of liquid measurements (pints, quarts, and gallons). In the eighteenth century, the English used two different gallons: the ale gallon

(282 cubic inches) and the wine gallon (231 cubic inches). The American colonists adopted the English wine gallon from the beginning and so it has remained.

But the English had to do *something* to punish the Americans for the Revolution, so they decided in 1824 to abandon their two-tier gallon system and to switch to the British Imperial gallon, which is equivalent to the volume of ten pounds of water at a temperature of 62 degrees Fahrenheit (or to put it more precisely if less memorably, the equivalent of the nice round number of 277.42 cubic inches).

The U.S. government decided not to switch and the result is that today Americans, shocked by the high price of petrol in Great Britain, are slightly relieved by getting a little more gasoline in an Imperial gallon. Joan Koenig, of the Office of Weights and Measures at the U.S. National Bureau of Standards, adds that the British are in the process of adopting the metric system, another indication that the Empire ain't what it used to be.

Submitted by Richard Speiss of Winnipeg, Manitoba.

Why Is That Piece of Tissue Paper Included in Wedding Invitations?

When wedding invitations come back from the printer, along comes a box of tissue paper that seems to serve no discernible purpose. Any prospective bride will tell you that one of the less than thrilling chores in the prewedding grind is hand-inserting a sheet of tissue paper inside each invitation. Why bother with the stuff?

According to Melanie Martini, associate editor of *Bride's* magazine, at one time the tissues did serve a practical purpose: to keep ink from smudging. Modern printing techniques have rendered the tissues obsolete in theory but not in practice. For some reason, that piece of tissue veritably reeks of class and tradition, so few brides leave it out.

Occasionally, brides at small weddings will use calligraphy on the invitations. In this case, the tissues might help blot the ink, as did the tissue papers of yore. But no less an authority than Elizabeth Post, in *Emily Post's Complete Book of Wedding*

Etiquette, says that the tissue paper may be discarded with impunity.

Submitted by Harrison Leon Church of Lebanon, Illinois.
Thanks also to Donna J. Budz of San Diego, California.

Why Does Neptune's Moon Triton Orbit "in Reverse?"

Our old astronomical all-star, Jeff Kanipe, associate editor of *Astronomy*, was willing to answer this Imponderable on the proviso that we made clear there is no such thing as "reverse" or "forward" in outer space, any more than there is an up and down. As usual, Jeff wrote such a clear and fascinating explanation that we'll let him speak for himself.

> In our solar system, most moons orbit their master planets in the same direction that the planets spin. If you could look down on Earth's north pole from space, you'd see that we rotate counterclockwise, from west to east. This is why the sun, moon, and stars seem to "rise" in the east and "set" in the west from Earth.
>
> The moon, too, orbits Earth west to east, although because we complete one rotation (one day) more quickly than the moon can complete a single orbit (about 27.3 days) it looks as if the moon is fixed in the sky. But if you note the moon's position over a few nights, you'll see that it moves eastward with respect to the stars. The planets also orbit the sun in a west-to-east direction as seen from the north pole of the solar system. Astronomers refer to this motion as "direct."
>
> Triton, Neptune's largest moon, doesn't orbit its master planet with a direct motion. Triton orbits in the direction opposite Neptune's spin and orbit. Astronomers think that a gravitational tug-of-war in the early solar system reversed Triton's orbit.
>
> Four and a half billion years ago, Triton was in its own orbit around the sun, and Neptune was in a slightly greater orbit just beyond Triton. Being the more massive of the pair, Neptune's

gravity pulled on Triton whenever the smaller planet passed by. Over millions of years, the distance between Neptune and Triton closed until Neptune exerted more gravitational influence on Triton than the sun.

Finally, during one orbit in which the two bodies passed particularly close to one another, Neptune's gravity wrenched Triton out of its orbit. Triton swung out ahead of Neptune and then fell back toward the planet along an elliptical orbit. That orbit, however, was in a clockwise direction, opposite the rotational spin and orbital direction of Neptune.

Submitted by Cheryl Topper of Brooklyn, New York.

Why Do Mis-hits of Golf Shots, Especially Irons, Sting So Badly and for So Long?

As if the pathetic trajectory of your ball weren't punishment enough, a mis-hit in golf is likely to be accompanied by a sustained stinging sensation in the hands. If a shot hurts, you either haven't struck the center of the ball or, even more likely, you haven't hit the ball with the sweet spot of the club. Dr. John R. McCarroll, of the Methodist Sports Medicine Center, explains:

> Hitting the toe or the heel of the club causes more stress to be sent up the shaft and radiated into the hand. It is essentially like holding on to a vibrating hammer or like being hit with a hammer on the hands because the stress comes up and causes the hands to absorb the shock.

John Story, of the Professional Golfers' Association of America, explains that not all golf clubs are alike when it comes to inflicting pain on the duffer. A mis-hit on a driver (or any other wood) is much more forgiving than the iron, which has a harder head and therefore creates much more vibration. The vibration from the mis-hit of a driver gets lost in the long shaft.

Dr. McCarroll adds that advances in club manufacturing have lessened the problem of hand stings: "The newer shafts such as graphite and casted clubs cause less pain to your hands than the classic forged club with a metal shaft."

Submitted by Ron Musgrove of San Leandro, California.

What Exactly Is Happening Physiologically When Your Stomach Growls?

You've got gas in your stomach even when you (and others) aren't aware of it. You swallow gas as you eat and drink, and as you continuously swallow saliva. Some gas lands in your stomach through bacterial fermentation.

Imagine your stomach and intestines as a front-loading washing machine in a laundromat. Instead of clothes, water, and detergent whooshing around, there are solid foods, liquids from your diet, water, digestive fluids, and gas constantly churning and contracting, even when you are not aware of it. This churning kneads and mixes the food and enzymes, making it easier for the stomach and intestines to digest and absorb the food.

But just as the excess water and suds must be eliminated from the washer, so must the food left in the stomach. These contractions enable the residue to move to the lower gut, where it is formed into feces.

Dr. Frank Davidoff, of the American College of Physicians, describes the arduous travels of gas in the stomach:

> Now when bubbles of gas and liquid are mixed together in a hollow, muscular tube and the tube contracts in waves, massaging the contents along the way, pushing portions of the mixture through narrow, contracted gut segments, the result is gurgling, splashing, and squeaking of all kinds—borborygmi, growls, rumblings—whatever you want to call them.
>
> Your stomach seems to growl more when you're hungry because part of the physiological condition of hunger is an increased muscular activity of your gut, as though it were anticipating the incoming meal, getting ready to move it along.

Of course, the washing machine metaphor breaks down just about now. The washing machine doesn't particularly care whether it continues to get fed, and unlike our stomachs, we're not constantly stuffing clothes, water, and detergent down its throat while it is still trying to work off its current load.

Submitted by Karen Lueck of Tulsa, Oklahoma. Thanks also to Ronald C. Semone of Washington, D.C.; Margaret MacDonald of San Francisco, California; Karl Valindras of Petaluma, California; and David A. Bohnke of Monroeville, Indiana.

Are You Ever Going to Answer the 12 Most Frequently Asked Irritating Questions?

A wise person once said: "There is no such thing as a stupid question." We would like to add a corollary. "Maybe, but there sure are some questions that we don't want to hear."

We are goodhearted by nature. We wake up in the morning with a smile on our face and love in our hearts. But nothing will turn our rosy optimism into irritability more than facing any of these UnImponderables.

There are only a few criteria for selecting Imponderables for these books:

1. They must present genuine mysteries that most people would not know the answer to.
2. The mysteries should deal with everyday life rather than esoteric, scientific, or philosophical questions.
3. They are "why" questions rather than who/what/where/when trivia questions.

WHY DO DOGS HAVE WET NOSES?

4. Seminormal people might be interested in the questions and answers.
5. They are mysteries that aren't easy to find the answer to, especially from books. Therefore, they are questions that shouldn't have been written about frequently.

Some of the most frequently asked Imponderables are ones that meet criteria one through four but fail miserably at number five. If someone else has answered them, they aren't really Imponderables anymore!

The bane of our existence is when a comedian like George Carlin, Steven Wright, or, worst of all, Gallagher, offers a witty rhetorical question. The result: One week later, our mailbox is stuffed with folks clamoring for an answer. And there is no way to answer these questions without denuding them of their humor or wit. When we try, we feel like academics trying to describe why the Marx Brothers are funny.

In the fervent, desperate hope that we can slow down to a trickle the flood of people asking these most frequently asked UnImponderables, we offer our quick answers to the following would-be Imponderables that aren't really Imponderables at all.

1. WHY *Do We Park on Driveways and Drive on Parkways?*

This is our least favorite UnImponderable, especially because we have already answered it ourselves in *Who Put the Butter in Butterfly?* We have graciously consented to allow us to quote our own answer:

> One of the main definitions of *way* is "a route or course that is or may be used to go from one place to another." New York's Robert Moses dubbed his "route or course that was used to go from one place to another" *parkway* because it was lined with trees and lawns in an attempt to simulate the beauty of a park. The *driveway*, just as much as a *highway* a *freeway*, or a *parkway*, is a path for automobiles. The driveway is a path, a *way* between the street and a house or garage.

2. IF 7-11 Stores Are Open 24 Hours, Why Do They Need Locks on the Doors?

Originally, 7-11 stores were open from 7:00 A.M. until 11:00 P.M., thus providing the name for the chain. Of course, these stores needed locks every day because they were used, logically enough, to lock the doors. But occasionally, locks are needed even in stores open 24 hours.

What if a single employee in a small-town location has to go to the bathroom? What if an urban store wants to provide security? What if the store is shut down because of an emergency, such as an earthquake? Locks come in handy.

3. WHY *Is There No Channel 1 on Televisions?*

Actually, at one time, there was a channel 1. But the FCC gave back the band to its original users—mobile radios. TV bands are much wider than radio bands; and as anyone who has a radio with TV-audio reception knows, the TV band is just an extension of the FM frequencies.

4. WHY *Does the Water Drain out of a Bathtub in a Counterclockwise Direction North of the Equator and Clockwise South of the Equator?*

Any physics book, astronomy book, or dictionary will give you the answer to this. The earth's rotation deflects moving bodies to the appropriate direction. This was discovered by nineteenth-century French engineer Gaspard de Coriolis.

The question is whether or not the Coriolis effect is strong enough to influence the spiraling of drains. Many other factors, such as wind patterns, the configuration and irregularities of the tub (in our tub, the water usually drains clockwise), and the circulation of the water as it fills the tank, affect the rotation of the drainage more.

Scientists have proven that water "remembers" its circulatory patterns long after it appears to be still. One scientist went to the effort of not draining water until it rested for eight days.

Under these conditions, M.I.T. physicist Ascher H. Shapiro found that the vortex repeatedly drained in a counterclockwise direction. His results were confirmed by a team at the University of Sydney, who found that the circular tub consistently drained clockwise "down under."

Most scientists agree that the Coriolis effect does not apply to the movements of larger bodies of water, such as rivers and streams. But one place you cannot confirm the Coriolis effect is in toilets. The force of the flush is much, much greater than the whimper of the Coriolis effect.

5. WHY *Can't We Tickle Ourselves?*

Psychologists have wrestled with this one since Freud but haven't really gotten very far. Many psychologists believe that elements of surprise, aggressiveness, and sexuality must be present to induce a laugh. As much as we may love ourselves, it isn't so easy to surprise ourselves with a tickle.

6. WHY *Is a Hamburger Called a "Hamburger" When It Doesn't Contain Ham?*

Because the dish isn't named after the meat but after the city where it was popularized—Hamburg, Germany.

7. WHY *Do Foreign Pop and Rock Performers Sing with an American Accent?*

Most of the early British superstars, such as John Lennon, Paul McCartney, and Mick Jagger, were ardent devotees of American blues and rhythm-and-blues singers. They consciously imitated the phrasing of their musical influences. Listen, by comparison, to the vocals of Peter Noone of Herman's Hermits or Gerry Marsden on "Ferry Cross the Mersey," and you'll see that not every British pop singer tried to repress his or her native accent.

Punk and new wave bands of the 1970s and 1980s made a

conscious attempt to assert their English diction and phrasing. One would never mistake the Sex Pistols, the Clash, or the Pet Shop Boys for American bands.

Performers on the European continent have found it tough to get any exposure on British or American radio without recording in English. So Scandinavian bands like Roxette, Abba, and A-Ha have taken the path of least resistance and recorded in English—in some cases, not even understanding the meaning of the lyrics they were singing.

8. WHY *Do Men Have Nipples?*

Some have argued that nipples are a vestigial organ, one that some time in our evolution may disappear altogether in men. The appendix is another organ that might have served a more important function in our bodies than it does today, where it exists mainly to provide high standards of living for surgeons.

Males actually have the anatomical equipment in place to provide milk, but it lies dormant unless stimulated by estrogen, the female hormone. Might men have suckled babies in the distant past?

9. WHY *Do They Carve Moons on Outhouse Doors?*

In his book *More of the Straight Dope*, Cecil Adams questions the premise of this often-asked Imponderable, and we side with him. There is no evidence to suggest that the custom preceded depictions of outhouse moons in cartoons, particularly Al Capp's "Li'l Abner." On occasion, recently built outhouses are "mooned" in the mistaken impression that a cherished tradition is being upheld.

Adams concludes his discussion with the most telling point. The question isn't so much why a moon is there as why a carving is on the outhouse: "The reason there's a hole in the first place is a lot simpler: it provides ventilation."

10. WHAT *Sadist Invented the Necktie? And What Supposed Function Did It Serve?*

This particular sadist wisely decided to remain anonymous. As for function, we have found no proof whatsoever that neckties ever had any purpose in life other than to look pretty. The Neckware Association of America agrees.

The modern necktie is a variation of the cravats first worn by Croatian mercenaries who took France by storm with their masochistic fashion statement in the seventeenth century. The English modified the French style and, typically, made ties as uncomfortable as possible, leading inevitably to the American Revolution.

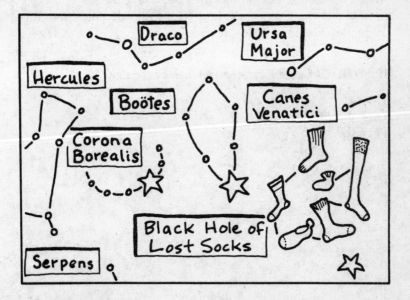

11. WHATEVER *Happened to the Missing Sock . . . ?*

If we could answer this question, we'd be in line for a Nobel prize and would be featured on "Sixty Minutes." No more being chained to the word processor.

But enough fantasy. We do have one theory that we will humbly propose. We lose pens all the time and find ourselves buying new ones constantly. But even though we wind up with single, unmatched socks in our drawers, we don't seem to replenish socks with the same rapidity as pens.

We had always assumed that we were losing socks caught on the sides of the washer or dryer. Callers on talk shows have proposed that socks meet, escape from the laundry room, and elope, never to be seen again. But the question nags . . . if they are disappearing one at a time, why don't we have to buy new socks all the time?

Maybe socks are mating in the washing machine but are actually giving birth to offspring during the spin cycle. Perhaps we are not losing socks but gaining one at a time.

Maybe we've been dealing with Imponderables and Un-Imponderables for a little too long.

12. WHICH *Came First, the Chicken or the Egg?*

The egg.
Then the chicken.
Then the sock.

Why Does the Phone Company Use that Obnoxious Three-Tone Signal before the Recording Tells You That They "Cannot Complete Your Call as Dialed"?

The phone company prefers to identify the three-tone signals as "Special Information Tones," but we like to call them "Ear-Splitting Shrieks from Hell." A busy signal sounds like the *Moonlight Sonata* compared to these ESSFHs.

AT&T's Dick Hofacker agrees with us on one point: these signals weren't meant for human consumption, but for machines with less sensitive auditory systems. Actually there are several different Special Information Tones, which serve different purposes:

> 1. They convey to fax and computerized calling systems (also known as automatic dialers) that they've dialed a nonworking number. Only after this message has been

conveyed to machines do humans, with ears now only semi-intact, learn from a synthesized voice machine that they've just wasted their call.

2. The phone company is capable of monitoring how many times the "cannot complete your phone call as dialed" message is reached. Phone companies monitor how often Special Information Tones are activated in any particular trunk of phone cables. If the count is high, it might be the first indication that a phone line has been severed.

3. The special information tone is capable of telling the phone company how many calls a given disconnected number attracts. While a phone company might reassign a residential phone number in three months, the former phone number of a big retail store might continue to attract calls for a year or more. By calculating the number of calls made to an "old" number, the phone company can accurately assess when to reassign the number to a new company.

4. A Special Information Tone also precedes the recording "All circuits are busy. Please try your call again later."

Even though each three-part Special Information Tone has a slightly different frequency and precedes a different announcement, in two ways they are uniform: They may not bother machines, but all the Ear-Shattering Shrieks from Hell are not going to be easy on your ears. And all of them will convey bad news. Wouldn't it be more humane to have the verbal recording precede the Ear-Splitting Shriek from Hell?

Submitted by Peter J. Mastrantuono of Woodbridge, New Jersey.

Why Do Doctors Always Advise Us to "Drink Plenty of Liquids" When We Have a Cold?

Has anyone ever told you *why* it is important to drink plenty of liquids when we have a cold? The simple answer is: to prevent dehydration.

Dr. Frank Davidoff, of the American College of Physicians in Philadelphia, was willing to tell us not only why we should all be good boys and girls and drink those liquids but why we get dehydrated in the first place, and why it is important not to be.

When we feel sick, we tend not to feel like eating or drinking, which can leave us dehydrated. But fever also causes water loss.

No, if your body temperature is two degrees higher than normal, water in your body doesn't evaporate noticeably faster. But fevers speed up the metabolism. As a result, you blow off more carbon dioxide and you need more oxygen to run your body, so you breathe faster. Every time you breathe you give off moisture. You are literally blowing off water, as well as "hot air" when you breathe, just as a whale's spout blows off water. Davidoff points out that "spit valves" on brass wind instruments are necessary in order to release condensed water because the air blown through the horns is so moist.

A high fever can be dangerous in and of itself, so the body tries to fight it off. The body's main defense is to evaporate moisture off and through the skin. Sometimes the moisture is imperceptible; sometimes it's a spritz (which is why we are usually sweaty when we have a fever); and other times, when a fever is finally breaking, it can be a drenching.

Drinking "plenty of liquids," then, is a way of replenishing the water lost by evaporation, sweating, and breathing. Medically, avoiding dehydration is especially important, as Davidoff explains:

Dehydration isn't a desirable state at any time, but in the presence of an infection, like a cold, it can be particularly aggravating, even dangerous.

1. Dehydration can make you feel generally bad, adding to the debility from the infection.

2. Dehydration can bring on or aggravate constipation; since bed rest and decreased food intake also cause constipation, this can be a bad combination.

3. Finally, and most important, dehydration thickens the mucus secretions from sinuses and bronchial passages. Thick secretions can block drainage from sinuses and lungs. Blocked drainage leads to discomfort and worsening infection in sinuses and to collapse of lung tissue and, worst of all, progressive infection in the lungs, which can become pneumonia.

Submitted by Daniel T. Placko Jr. of Chicago, Illinois.

Why Do Colored Soaps and Shampoos Yield White Suds?

Judging from our mail, this Imponderable is Uppermost on the minds of our readers lately. God knows why, but it is.

Here's the scoop. Very little dye is put into soap or shampoo to color them. As College of San Mateo physics professor Donald Beaty puts it, "When it's in the bottle, the light that is used to view the liquid passes through a considerable thickness of colorful shampoo or liquid soap." But once you make suds, the water-soluble dye is highly diluted. The percentage of dyed color contained in the original product is greatly reduced. Beaty adds that nothing magical "happens" to the colorant in the dye:

Light that reflects from the surface of each soap bubble will contain the same ranges of colors as the light used to illuminate the lather. We tend to perceive the reflected light as white light if the incident light is normal room light or daylight.

Sally Miller, a consumer services representative of soap and shampoo behemoth Procter & Gamble Company, told *Imponderables* that manufacturers could easily put enough colorant into bar soaps or shampoos to yield colored suds, but their research indicates that "most consumers find white lather preferable for applying to the skin or the hair." A high concentration of dye could also stain towels and turn a demure blonde Prell user into a green-haired Cyndi Lauper lookalike.

Submitted by Dave Calicchia of West Palm Beach, Florida. Thanks also to Mary Cannon, of Chandler, Arizona; Barry Rhodes, Gene Mace, and Jim Hill of Ucon, Idaho; Jodie Masnick of Howell, New Jersey; Danny Brown of Flora, Illinois; Steve Altig of Las Vegas, Nevada; Johanna Tiefenbach of Waldron, Saskatchewan; and Nancy Fukuda of Monterey, California.

Why Do Most People Wear Wristwatches on Their Left Hand?

At first, we thought: This is obvious. Most people are right-handed and use the right arm more often than the left. Therefore, they are more likely to damage the watch while wearing it on their dominant hand.

We spoke to several experts about the subject, including horologist Henry Fried, Bulova's Pat Campbell, and Lowell Drutman of Timex. They concurred with our theory but added a couple of their own. "Have you ever seen a right-handed person trying to buckle up a leather strap on his right wrist?" asked Drutman. "They aren't very successful." Try it. He's right.

But all three also offered another theory that helps explain why many left-handers wear their watches on their left hands, too. Ever since the days of the pocket watch, the stem (the round part you wind) has been placed adjacent to the "3" (on the right-hand side of the watch). This location makes it awkward to wind the clock with the left hand, whether you are left-handed, right-handed, or ambidextrous. Whether generations of windless watches will change wrist preferences is a matter for sociologists of the future to keep tabs on.

Fried reports that no watchmaker has ever tried to market a "left-hander's" watch, although an occasional iconoclastic designer has placed the stem on the "9" side.

Submitted by Margaret McCallion of Londonderry, New Hampshire. Thanks also to Jim LaBelle of South Bend, Indiana, and Sharon Roberts of Amos, Quebec.

What Do the Grades of Eggs Signify? What's the Difference Between "A" and "AA" Eggs?

We get frustrated when we can't find answers to Imponderables, but sometimes we are driven nuts when we are provided too much information. The USDA sent us several healthy-sized handbooks on egg grading, and they were as hard to decipher as the instruction booklets that come with VCRs.

These handbooks are serious affairs. the first page of one of them provides definitions of words and terms used throughout the book, esoteric words like "person" (defined as "any individual, partnership, association, business trust, corporation, or any organized group of persons, whether incorporated or not") and "quality" ("the inherent properties of any product which determine its relative degree of excellence"). You get the idea. So when answering this Imponderable, it was no mean feat to separate the shell from the egg white here, and that is no yolk.

Most of the eggs sold over the counter in supermarkets are

"AA" grade, the highest distinction. The next grade is "A," followed by "B." "C," the victim of grade inflation, has been phased out. Eggs must pass criteria in four different categories before they can receive the "AA" grade:

1. Shell—Both "A" and "AA" grades must have clean, unbroken shells with a "practically normal appearance." "B" quality eggs may be slightly stained ($\frac{1}{32}$ of the surface if localized, or $\frac{1}{16}$ if scattered). Grade "B" eggs may be abnormally shaped or have a ridge or thin spots.

2. The air cell—The air cell is the space between the shell membranes that is usually found in the large end of an egg. When an egg is held large end up, the depth of the air cell can't exceed $\frac{1}{8}''$ in a grade "AA," $\frac{3}{16}''$ in a grade "A," and $\frac{3}{16}''$ in a grade "B."

3. Egg Whites—Grade "AA" eggs must have a clear and firm white. Grade "A" whites must be clear and "reasonably firm" with a "fairly well-defined yolk outline when the egg is twirled." Grade "B" eggs not only can appear weak and watery but can contain small blood and meat spots.

4. Yolks—"AA" yolks stand up tall and blend into the surrounding white. "A" yolks are round and upstanding and have a more discernible outline. Grade "B" yolks are enlarged and flatted and marred with germ development.

Egg grades have nothing to do with egg size. A pee wee with a relatively small air cell will receive an "AA" while a jumbo with a flat yolk will get a low passing "B."

How are they tested? While eggs used to be graded by hand candling, most inspections are now done by machine.

Submitted by Eric Borgos of Northampton, Massachusetts. Thanks also to Rick DeWitt of Erie, Pennsylvania.

Since Blood is Red, Why Do Veins Look Blue?

We got into trouble with some readers when we gave a slightly facetious explanation of the expression "blue-blooded" in *Who Put the Butter in Butterfly?*, so we'll play it straight here. In fact, we'll let one of our favorite medical authorities, Dr. Frank Davidoff, associate executive vice-president of the American College of Physicians, take the floor:

> Veins look blue because they are fairly large blood vessels, full of blood that has been stripped of its oxygen load, and close enough to the surface of your skin to see the blue color of this blood.
>
> Inside the red blood cells that make up about 40% of your blood volume is the oxygen carrying pigment called hemoglobin. As the red cells pass through your lungs, the hemoglobin picks up oxygen and binds it, turning bright red in the process. The oxygen-hemoglobin combination is called "oxyhemoglobin." This oxyhemoglobin is pumped on out of your heart under pressure through the large muscular blood vessels called arteries.
>
> Out in the tissues, red cells with their oxyhemoglobin ultimately pass on through tiny blood vessels called capillaries, where they give up their oxygen to cells for use in metabolism. (The skin is rich in capillaries, which is why healthy, non-pigmented skin is pink; a sudden rush of extra oxyhemoglobin into dilated blood vessels in skin causes the phenomenon of blushing).
>
> As hemoglobin loses its oxygen, it turns a dark purplish blue —deoxyhemoglobin—which collects in larger and larger veins on its way back to the heart. While the biggest veins are deep in the tissues (they tend to run paired with the largest arteries), some fairly large veins lie just under the skin, where you can appreciate their blueness if there isn't too much brown skin pigment (melanin) to hide the color.

Submitted by Mrs. R. D. Harvey of Gulf Breeze, Florida. Thanks also to Jae Hoon Chung of Demarest, New Jersey, and Ron Pateman of Chicago, Illinois.

Why Does Just About Everything Look Darker When it Gets Wet?

Come to think of it, reader Russell has a point. Drop some water on your new cream-colored blouse and you get a dark spot. Have a clod standing near you spill his Perrier on your navy blue blazer and the light liquid somehow manages to make the coat's dark color even darker. Why is this so?

Elementary physics, it turns out. You lose the true color of the garment in three ways:

1. Even a thin coating of water will force light coming toward the garment to refract within the water film. The available light is thus disbursed.

2. The reflection on the surface of the water itself causes incoherent light scattering.

3. A combination of the two points above ensures that there will be less light available on the surface of the jacket to reflect back to your eyes. Thus the spot will appear darker than the rest of the jacket that doesn't have to compete with water in order to reflect light.

Submitted by Kathleen Russell of Grand Rapids, Michigan. Thanks also to Kent Parks of Raleigh, North Carolina.

Why Is the American Thanksgiving on Thursday? Was the Original Thanksgiving on Thursday?

Although latter-day cynics might conclude that Thanksgiving was set on Thursday in order to wangle a four-day weekend, little evidence supports that. In fact, we don't know what day of the week the Plymouth Colony's first Thanksgiving was celebrated.

But we do know that Plymouth's first Thanksgiving was held in mid-October, 1621, and lasted three days. Other colonies held their Thanksgiving celebrations on different days of the week. And all the colonies occasionally declared one-shot thanksgivings on varying days of the week following special blessings or tragedies in their communities.

In 1668, the Plymouth General Court declared that November 25 be declared an annual day of thanksgiving. This proclamation lasted all of five years.

Most New England colonies held their own thanksgivings on either Wednesday or Thursday, probably to distance the holidays from the Sabbath. Colonists were, appropriately enough, puritanical about intruding upon the Sabbath in any way, so not only was Sunday ruled out, but so were the day of preparation (Saturday) and the day after (Monday). Friday was a fast day of the Catholic church, and the Puritans wanted no connection or identification with Catholic practices.

Thursday was known in Boston and a few other northeastern towns as "lecture day", when ministers gave religious lectures in the afternoon. Since some citizens were already taking time away from their work to attend these meetings, perhaps "lecture day" was the reason Thursday beat out Wednesday as the popular choice for Thanksgiving.

The first *national* Thanksgiving celebrated the American victory over the British at Saratoga in 1777. Samuel Adams prevailed upon the Continental Congress to declare a day of thanksgiving. But several colonies continued to celebrate their local versions as well.

George Washington issued the first presidential proclamation of Thanksgiving, designating Thursday, November 26, 1789, as the day of celebration. With the exception of John Adams' attempt at one Wednesday Thanksgiving on May 9, 1798, all national Thanksgiving days since 1789 have been celebrated cn Thursday.

But no uniform date was selected for Thanksgiving until Abraham Lincoln declared that starting in 1863, the last Thursday in November would be the national day. His proclamation was motivated by not only the Union's victory in the Civil War but the pressure exerted by the passionate editorials of women's magazine editor Sarah Josepha Hale, who relentlessly promoted the issue for over 35 years. Lincoln never stated why he chose Thursday, but presumably he was following the tradition of the Puritans and, later, George Washington.

For some reason, presidents haven't been able to stop tinkering with the date of Thanksgiving. Andrew Johnson experimented with the first Thursday of December, 1865, as a new date. Johnson relented and returned to Lincoln's last Thursday in November the next year, but he was impeached anyway. Ulysses S. Grant preferred the third Thursday in November, 1869. Seventy years later, Franklin Delano Roosevelt pulled a U.S. Grant and proclaimed Thursday, November 23, rather than November 30, as Thanksgiving Day.

But traditions were too settled by then. Many states observed Thanksgiving on the last Thursday anyway. FDR and Congress eventually cooperated on a joint resolution placing Thanksgiving on the fourth Thursday in November. Ever since, not even Richard Nixon has tried to move it.

Submitted by Rick DeWitt of Erie, Pennsylvania. Thanks also to Richard Miranda of Renton, Washington.

Why Are the Valve Stems on Fire Hydrants Pentagonal?

We were confronted with this Imponderable on a radio show, and we asked if any listeners had ever seen a pentagonal wrench. The answer: square wrenches, sure; hexagonal wrenches, of course. But a five-sided wrench? Nope.

We should have figured it out. Fire hydrants with five-sided valve stems were designed precisely because pentagonal wrenches are not generally distributed. Since only fire hydrants require five-sided wrenches, the general population doesn't own them.

And more specifically, vandals don't own them. Even van-

WHY DO DOGS HAVE WET NOSES?

dals have discovered you can't easily open a five-sided valve stem if you are using a square or hexagonal wrench.

Not that the lack of proper tools has kept vandals from trying. New York City firefighter Brenda Berkman told *Imponderables* that kids use conventional monkey wrenches of all kinds to try to open hydrants during the summer. Even when they don't succeed in opening the hydrants, they sometimes strip the nuts. David Cerull, president of the Fire Collectors Club, adds that some cities are installing special collars around the valve stem to keep vandals away.

Why Are Most Receipts from Cash Registers Printed in Purple?

According to Robin Pierce, business products division manager of Citizen CBM American Corp., the answer, appropriately enough for a cash register, concerns the preservation of cold cash. Purple ink, because of the chemical constituents that make up the oil base, has a longer life than any other color. The longer the ink lasts, the longer the purple ribbons last, and the more money the shopkeepers save.

And those of us who have the propensity for arriving at the checkout line of a supermarket at precisely the time when the checker decides to change ribbons also applaud the idea of long-lasting ink, be it purple or chartreuse.

Submitted by Joseph Blake, Jr. of Ottawa, Kansas.

HOW Do Kangaroos Clean Their Pouches?

If you think the illustration above is a bit gross, consider the actual answer. According to Rick Barongi, curator of mammals at the Sans Diego Zoo, kangaroos use their forefeet to open their pouches wide and then proceed to stick their heads in and lick their pouches clean!

After the mother gives birth, keeping the pouch clean requires some effort, for joeys stay in the pouch for many months (up to seven or eight months for the largest kangaroos). After that, joeys pop out for walks and a snack but return to the mother's pouch when hungry. The joeys will continue to enter the pouch until they can no longer squeeze into it or their mothers no longer make them welcome.

Exactly what is the mother cleaning out of her pouch? Miles Roberts, deputy head of research at the National Zoological Park, told us that along with the expected epidermis flakes that accumulate, a waxy substance forms in the pouch that the kangaroos try to lick off. When the pouch is occupied by her joey, the mother's cleaning activity increases; not only does mom have to lick off the usual debris but also the joey's droppings.

And to think we complain about changing diapers.

Submitted by Terri Rippey of Saint Joseph, Missouri.

Why Aren't All Beer Bottle Caps Twistoffs? Are There Any Advantages to Nontwistoff Caps?

Yes, there is one disadvantage to twistoff caps. You may have noticed that with rare exceptions, bottles without twistoff caps are imports. Twistoffs are made out of aluminum, a soft metal. L. Van Munching, Jr., of Van Munching & Co., U.S. distributors of Heineken beer, told *Imponderables* that soft caps can be loosened in transit with the danger of beer and/or air leaking out of the bottle.

But Phil Katz, of the Beer Institute, says that the domestic beer industry has found few problems with twistoff caps. Consumers have a strong preference for twistoffs, and since they cost no more than conventional closures, the domestic beer industry has been happy to comply.

Much of the impetus for the twistoff technology came from bottle manufacturers. After can manufacturers developed the pull tab for their containers, consumers no longer wanted to bother with the inconvenience of bottle or can openers. The bottle industry needed to offer a cap that could be opened with the hands or risk losing even more market share to aluminum cans.

Why Won't the Contents of a 13-Ounce Bag of Coffee Fit into a 16-Ounce Coffee Can?

This Imponderable is less theoretical than it may seem at first, since "gourmet" coffee packaged in 13-ounce bags has become a popular item. Consumers like the security of storing coffee in a sturdy, tightly closed coffee can. But they become frustrated when they can't fit the bag's 13-ounces of coffee into a container that will supposedly hold three ounces more. Have coffee sellers been ripping us off with undersize containers all these years? And how could the original pound of coffee fit into the 16-ounce can if it now will not hold 13 ounces of the bagged coffee?

The answer, says John Adinolfi, of the National Coffee Association of U.S.A., has nothing to do with fraud and a lot to do with "density":

> The 13-ounce bag may contain coffee with a much lower density than the coffee packed in the 16-ounce can. This may be especially true if the coffee was processed utilizing a newer "fast roast" technique which produces a much lower density. In addition, in the packaging process, ground coffee is vibrated vigorously to compact it so it can be packaged efficiently.

Bridget A. MacConnell, of General Foods, adds that a vacuum is drawn on coffee bags, which acts to further compress the coffee:

> When you open the vacuum bag and pour the coffee out, you reduce the density of the coffee as you pour it—the agitation loosens it. If you tap the can after you've poured the coffee in, that will reduce the level somewhat, but probably not enough to fit the entire 13 ounces.

Many coffee cans have been downsized from 16 ounces to 13 ounces. Perhaps coffee marketers have been decreasing the size of their cans to help stamp out this Imponderable, but somehow we have a gut feeling that might not have been their primary motivation.

Submitted by Carolyn Ehrlich of Little Neck, New York.

How Do Men Produce Falsetto Voices?

We received a nifty response from Dr. Michael J. D'Asaro, a speech pathologist in Santa Monica, California:

> Falsetto voice, which is the highest portion of the pitch range, is produced by an extreme contraction of the laryngeal muscles and elevation of the larynx, permitting only a very short segment of the vocal cords to vibrate, a portion furthest forward in the length of the vocal cords.
>
> The rest of the vocal cords are held stationary and the short segment that vibrates vibrates at an extremely high frequency, as do shorter strings in musical instruments.

Singers can be trained to drift from their usual pitches into the falsetto range without interrupting the vibration, but D'Asaro says that in the untrained voice, "there is often a break in vibration similar to the voice breaks associated with voice change in males at puberty."

Why Don't You Ever Hear Women Singing Falsetto?

We pride ourselves on the fact that we don't find interesting facts in books or magazines and then build Imponderables around them. We always start with genuine mysteries and then try to find the answers.

This Imponderable is the first one we've ever used that was sent in by a source. Dr. D'Asaro added this tidbit as a sidebar to his answer to the last Imponderable. But since we had never thought about this question before, and wish we had, and since we had no idea of the answer, we'll break precedent:

... there is no counterpart to falsetto in the female voice. The female vocal mechanism, being much smaller than the male, naturally vibrates at a higher frequency. It typically can vibrate no higher than the soprano range, although there are a few notable exceptions in singers with extreme ranges.

Submitted by Dr. Michael J. D'Asaro of Santa Monica, California.

What Unit of Measurement Is Indicated by the Numbers on Nonreal-Time Counters on VCRs and Audio Tape Recorders? Are the Settings Uniform on the Recorders of Different Companies?

Now that new taping equipment usually comes with electronic rather than mechanical counters, we don't understand why every recorder isn't equipped with a real-time counter. On VCRs, for example, if you know the length of the first of two shows you have taped, with a real-time counter you can stop the tape at the exact point where the second show begins. God forbid we should have to endure the major strain of reversing and fast-forwarding with our remote control to find a program!

Consultation with our electronics experts gave us the expected response. The counters on VCRs and audio tape recorders are not calibrated for any specific length of time. And the settings are not uniform from company to company. As TDK's Robert Fontana puts it: "Switching to another tape deck with index numbers logged from another will likely render havoc. Consistency and compatibility are not virtues of such counters."

In fact, the counters on recorders vary from machine to machine within the same company. And we have learned from painful experience that a count of 100 at the beginning of the tape doesn't signify the same amount of time as 100 at the end of the tape. Fontana summarizes: "Counters serve no purpose other than to index what's on the tape when that tape deck is used."

What Determines Whether a Letter with Insufficient Postage Will Be Sent to the Addressee or Back to the Sender?

Believers in Murphy's Law assume that the rule of thumb is: If *I* sent the letter with insufficient postage, I'll get it back; but if I'm the addressee, *I'll* get it back. But why go through life with such a paranoiac attitude? If there is anything we can trust in this world, even more than Murphy's Law, it is that our postal system will have a rule and regulation concerning every possible eventuality.

In general, the policy is simple. If there is postage affixed to a letter or parcel, but it is insufficient, the mail will be "promptly dispatched" to the addressee postage due. If the addressee agrees to pay the discrepancy, all is fine with the world. If the addressee refuses payment, the mail is returned to the sender who must, on first-class mail, pay the additional postage due and remail the piece. Senders of any other class must pay not only the deficiency but the forwarding postage, if any, and the return postage.

Many letters are sent bearing no postage whatsoever. In some cases, the stamps have fallen off. Others go naked because of neglect or forgetfulness. These pieces are marked "returned for postage" and returned to the sender.

The USPS has had difficulty in the past with jerks trying to send mail without having to pay for the privilege. A common method of freeloaders is deliberately to not affix a stamp and to reverse the address and the return address, hoping that the mail will be "returned" to the intended recipient. But sometimes even the most innocent person forgets to affix a stamp on an envelope without a return address. The postal system is cracking down on fraud, so the innocent person won't get his letter delivered. According to the *Domestic Mail Manual* of the USPS,

> If no return address is shown, or if the delivery and return address are identical, or if it is determined that the delivery address and the return address, while different, are actually for the same person or organization, the piece will be disposed of . . .

The *Domestic Mail Manual* covers all kinds of contingencies that even *Imponderables* readers might not think about. For example, what if an absentminded person accidentally slips her "prepaid" Federal Express package into a USPS collection box? The post office is actually kind enough to call its competitor and say, "Yo! We've got business for you. You have until the close of the next workday to pick it up." If Federal Express doesn't pick it up (not too likely), the USPS returns it to the sender postage due.

Ah, but what postage fee should they charge? Luckily for the sender, they charge first-class rather than Express Mail prices:

> Compute the postage-due amount from the point at which the unpaid matter entered the mailstream to the sender's location. If the entry point is unknown, compute the postage due from where the matter was first found in the mailstream to the sender's location. . . . Do not deliver such mail to the addressee, or provide address-correction or forwarding service.

And what happens when the post office damages a stamp or envelope? It depends upon whether the envelope has already been canceled. If it is apparent to postal workers from the cancellation that a stamp once was affixed to the envelope, the piece is treated as if the stamp were still there.

And what happens if you buy some stamps that aren't sticky enough to stay on an envelope? Or those stamps you bought during a heat wave have curled up because of humidity? The

USPS will gladly exchange stamps at full value, "but only for an equal number of stamps of the same denomination. . . . Each such transaction is further limited to stamps with a total value of $100 or less from each customer."

Submitted by Paula Chaffee of Utica, Michigan.

Why Does the Cold Water That Comes Out of the Bathroom Faucet Seem Colder than the Cold Water from the Kitchen Faucet?

The operative word in the question is "seem." All of our plumbing experts claimed that it just ain't so.

Gary Felsinger, marketing manager of the faucets and fittings division of Kohler Co., offered a few plausible theories: "Water temperature could be affected by the length of pipe run, the type of insulation, and perhaps heating ducts that are many times installed under the cabinet where the kitchen sink is installed." But these conditions would only affect a tiny fraction of homes and apartments.

Jim Datka, of American Standard, mentioned to us that bathroom water faucets tend to get used more often than kitchen faucets. Perhaps the posers of this Imponderable were working with an already cold water faucet in the bathroom? Or were seeking cold water after having run hot water—perhaps after doing the dishes?

Plumbers we spoke to tended to pooh-pooh the premise of this Imponderable. They all pointed out that water in the house comes from one source, and that the water is at the same temperature when it enters the house.

The experts' explanations make sense to the Mr. Spock in us, but not to our Scotty. Because, darn it, the cold water in our bathroom *does* seem colder than the cold water in our kitchen.

Readers, is the cold water colder in your bathroom than in your kitchen? Does anybody have any theories to explain either the reality or the perception of this only semi-resolved Imponderable?

Submitted by Joni E. Ray, Karen K. Kinonen, and Bill M. Quillard of Vancouver, Washington. Thanks also to Caroline Corenzo, of Worcester, Massachusetts.

Is There any Particular Reason Why Boats and Airplanes Have Red Lights on the Left Side and Green Lights on the Right?

The origins of this practice are obscure. Wayne Young, of the Marine Board of the National Research Council, suggests that side lights might be a descendant of the system originally used for hand buoys. As far back as 1889, the International Marine Conference agreed on a uniform coloring system, subsequently changed by a League of Nations subcommittee in 1936 to the current Uniform System of black buoys with green or white lights on the starboard side and red buoys with red or white lights on the port side.

In practice, the color scheme of side lights makes right-of-way decisions a snap for pilots or navigators, using color associations we have all known since childhood. B. Scott Coe, of *Sail* magazine, explains the "stop and go" theory:

Picture a four-way stop. The boat to your right has the right of way. Looking at him, you see his left, or port side, which shows a red light. This means you stop, he goes. Presumably he sees your green (starboard) light and will go. If you look at the boat on the left of you at the crossing, you see his green light. This means you go and he stops. Presumably, that boat is seeing your red (port) light and will stop. An old sailing ditty goes: 'If to starboard red appear, 'tis your duty to keep clear.'

Side lights also enable airplanes and ships to pass each other in the dark. Rexford B. Sherman, director of research and information services at the American Association of Port Authorities, wrote *Imponderables* that he believes:

> the explanation lies with navigational "rules of the road" that require ships or aircraft to pass each other on the right side. Thus the position of the lights vis-a-vis an approaching vessel or airplane would indicate whether your craft is properly positioned in relation to the other.
>
> Of course, air traffic controllers endeavor to prevent planes from passing each other too closely. Still, the side lights, which can be seen from a surprisingly long range, enable a plane to detect the presence and flight direction of nearby aircraft.

Submitted by Wally De Vasier of Fairfield, Virginia. Thanks also to Andrew Kass of Staten Island, New York.

How Do They Get the Mint Flavoring on Toothpicks?

Long ago, toothpick manufacturers decided that hand-rolling toothpicks in mint flavoring might be a tad labor-intensive. So they spray the flavor on the toothpicks.

Submitted by Elizabeth L. Wendling of Richfield, Ohio.

What Is the "Bias" Referred to in High Bias Audio Tape? Is High Bias Superior to Low Bias?

We heard from Robert Fontana, customer/technical service manager of tape giant TDK Electronics Corp.:

In layman's language, bias is a technical term that describes the ultrasonic signal that is mixed with the audio signal during recording. Its purpose is to facilitate a high fidelity recording onto magnetic tape. The absence of bias would yield a recording that sounds substantially inferior to the source.

High bias and low bias are . . . descriptions of the amount of bias required to make a good recording onto tape. Different tape formulations require different amounts of bias. Hence, normal bias, high bias, and metal bias denote different types of tape formulations whose bias requirements are different.

A high bias recording has a higher voltage signal applied than the normal bias type.

William J. Goffi, of Maxell, told *Imponderables* that high bias tapes capture more highs and lows than normal bias tape, and is generally more sensitive. This sensitivity makes it the proper choice for recording music, while low bias tape is usually sufficient for capturing voice.

Submitted by Jim Kowald of Green Bay, Wisconsin.

What Precisely Is Sea Level? And How Do They Determine Exactly What It Is?

Painstakingly. Obviously, the sea level in any particular location is constantly changing. If you measure the ocean during low tide and then high tide, you won't come up with the same figure. Wind and barometric shifts also affect the elevation of the seas.

But the oceans are joined and their height variation is slight. So geodesists (mathematicians who specialize in the study of measurement) and oceanographers settle for an approximation. Because the cliché that "water seeks its own level" is true, geodesists worry more about sea level variations over time than between places. Measurements are taken all over the globe;

there is no one place where sea level is determined. One sea level fits all.

The National Geodetic Survey defines "mean sea level" as the "average location of the interface between ocean and atmosphere, over a period of time sufficiently long so that all random and periodic variations of short duration average to zero." The U.S. National Ocean Service has set 19 as the appropriate number of years to sample sea levels to eliminate such variations; in some cases, measurements are taken on an hourly basis. Geodesists simply add up the 19 years of samples and divide by 19 to arrive at the mean sea level.

The mean sea level has been rising throughout most of the twentieth century—on average, over a millimeter a year. On a few occasions, sea level has risen as much as five or six millimeters in a year, not exactly causing flood conditions, but enough to indicate that the rise was caused by melting of glaciers. If theories of the greenhouse effect and global warming are true, the rise of the global sea level in the future will be more than the proverbial drop in the bucket.

Submitted by Janice Brown of Albany, Oregon. Thanks also to Wendy Neuman of Plaistow, New Hampshire; Noel Ludwig of Littleton, Colorado; Jay Howard Horne of Pittsburgh, Pennsylvania; Charles F. Longaker of Mentor, Ohio; and Mrs. Violet Wright of Hobbes, New Mexico.

Why Do Basketballs Have Fake Seams? Do They Have a Practical Purpose or Are They Merely Decorative?

A caller on a radio talk show asked this question indignantly, as if the ball industry were purposely perpetrating a fraud, at worst, and foisting unnecessary decoration on a ball, at best. Before you accuse basketball manufacturers of making a needless fashion statement, consider that most basketball players need all the help they can get manipulating a basketball. A basketball is too big for all but the Kareems and Ewings of the world to grasp with their fingers. Those "fake" seams are there to help you grip the ball (similarly, quarterbacks make sure their fingers make contact with the seams when passing).

Basketball manufacturers make two kinds of seams, narrow and wide. National Basketball Association professionals prefer the narrow-channel seams, while many amateurs, particularly young people with small hands, use wide-channel seams.

Why Are Lakes Windier at Midday than During Morning or Night?

Richard Williams, a meteorologist at the National Weather Service's National Severe Storms Forecast Center, has actually paid cash money to buy *Imponderables* books (we knew there was something we like about him), and sent in his own Imponderables in the past. And now he was kind enough to send us a detailed letter on the subject at hand.

Williams emphasizes that it is windier over land as well as lake during midday. However, the wind increase is accentuated over the relatively smooth, open surface of a lake.

> Often, the lowest layers of the atmosphere are at rest during the night and more active or turbulent by day. At night, particularly on clear nights, the earth's surface cools along with the adjacent lowest layers of the atmosphere. The lower layers cool faster than the higher layers, producing a "stable" temperature regime with cool air at ground level and relatively warmer air above the surface.
>
> Under these conditions a temperature inversion will form a few hundred feet above the earth's surface. An inversion is a vertical zone in which temperatures rise with increasing altitude ver-

sus the normal cooling. The inversion serves as a barrier or boundary—separating the near-surface air from wind flow aloft. Often at night, calm or very light wind flow will occur at ground level even though the winds aloft continue with little change in speed from day to night.

After sunrise, if the day is sunny or at least partially so, the sun warms the ground. In the lowest layers of the atmosphere, warm, turbulent mixing occurs and the inversion boundary disappears. Once this happens, the general wind flow resumes at the surface. Winds that were probably present during the night just a few hundred feet above the surface can again be felt at ground level. *The midday increase in winds is most pronounced over water where there is less resistance to wind flow.*

Another effect occurs along a coastline and over large lakes. Above a large body of water, local land-to-water wind circulations develop due to the unequal heating of water and land surfaces. This differential heating during the afternoon produces a water-to-land breeze, known as the sea breeze or lake breeze. At night a weaker land-to-water low level breeze can occur: the land breeze.

Submitted by C. Loewenson of New York, New York.

Why Does Wool Obtain Its "Distinctive" Smell When It Gets Wet?

"Distinctive," heh. What delicacy of expression.

When alive, all sheep manufacture lanolin, a secretion from the sebaceous glands—the equivalent of human perspiration. Lanolin collects in the wool and prevents it from drying out. That's the good news. But the bad news is that lanolin helps impart the "distinctive" smell of sheep when they get wet.

Almost all of the lanolin should be removed in the processing of wool. After wool is sheared and graded, the next step is the washing and scouring of the fibers. The wool runs through a series of rakes that comb out foreign material and a series of tubs filled with a detergent solution. After the wool is cleaned, it passes through several water rinses that remove the lanolin. Then the wool passes through squeeze rolls and is hot-air dried.

If the scouring process is insufficient, too much lanolin may be retained in the wool. Or if the chemicals used in the scouring process are too strong, it may degrade the fibers. Both problems could cause smelly products.

Our guess is that your question refers to a bulky wool sweater rather than, say, a pair of worsted pants. Representatives of The Wool Bureau and the American Wool Council both mentioned "oil wool" as the likely inspiration for this Imponderable.

Oil wool is intentionally not totally scoured in processing because the natural grease makes knitting easier. The famous Aran Island sweaters of Ireland are notorious "stinkers." Note that wool overcoats usually don't have a problem when it rains because modern scouring and finishing technology remove virtually all of the wool's lanolin.

Submitted by Pierre Jelenc of New York, New York.

Why Does the Groom Carry the Bride over the Threshold?

With the price of housing being what it is today, we think it might be more appropriate to have the real estate broker carry both the bride and groom over the threshold of their new home.

This superstitious countercharm dates back to the Romans, who believed that spirits resided at a home's entrance. Stephanie de Lys, in her book *A Treasury of American Superstitions*, writes that the Romans believed good and evil spirits slugged it out at the threshold. They also believed that if one walked into the house with the left foot first, evil would triumph; if the right foot came first, the good spirits would predominate. So why don't the bride and groom simply take care to put their right foot forward when entering their new abode?

Those Romans were just a tad sexist, as de Lys explains: "The groom, knowing that a woman in a highly emotional state is very apt to be careless, took no chances, and picked her up in his arms and carried her into the house."

Submitted by Marge Fener of Hempstead, New York.

Why Is There Aluminum Foil on the Neck of Champagne Bottles?

According to Irving Smith Kogan of the Champagne Association, the aluminum foil is there to cover up the less than thrillingly attractive wiring that helps keep the cork under pressure (the French word for the wire is *muselet*, which means "muzzle").

Before the days of aluminum foil, lead was used to cover the wire muzzle. Kogan adds that triangular "weep holes" were added to rid the lead of condensation. Even now, some champagne makers add triangular- or diamond-shaped holes to the foil for decorative purposes and as a nod to tradition.

The muzzle was a late nineteenth-century addition to champagne making. Before then, corks were hammered into place and secured by hand-tied twine.

We had heard a rumor that the foil was there to obscure the occasional bottle of champagne that had a short fill. But Kogan assured us that in this high-tech age, the possibility of a short fill is highly unlikely. Champagne is given its dosage injection at the same table where the cork is inserted. There isn't enough time for the champagne to bubble away.

What Kind of Container Holds the Rain Measured by Meteorologists?

You can set a bucket outside in your backyard, let the precipitation accumulate, and measure the bucket with a ruler. But after a while the thought is likely to occur to you: How big is the container supposed to be? Sure, it will take more rain to fill an inch of a big bucket than a thin beaker, but then the larger circumference of the bucket will also trap more water. Hmmmm. This isn't as simple as it first seemed.

It turns out that meteorologists don't let this stuff worry them too much. They use many different devices to measure rainfall. Perhaps the most common is the eight-inch rain gauge, a simple metal cylinder with an eight-inch-diameter top. The water is funneled from the outside cylinder into a smaller inner gauge. The water in the inner gauge is measured by a calibrated wooden or metal stick (which can convert the contents of different-sized gauges into the "inches" we hear about in weather reports). By funneling the water into the narrow inner gauge, the vertical scale is expanded, allowing accurate reading of rainfall to the nearest hundredth of an inch.

Richard Williams, meteorologist for the National Weather Service, told *Imponderables* that most of his agency's offices use another method: weighing rain in a bucket and using a mathematical formula to convert weight into hundredths.

Williams adds that in a third type of gauge, rainfall is not collected at all:

> As it falls, each one-hundredth inch of precipitation fills a small metal "bucket.'" The bucket fills, tips over, and then empties.

Each fill/empty cycle triggers an electrical contact and the number of "tips" is charted to determine the rainfall. This is particularly useful in determining the rate of rainfall and in making a permanent chart of the event.

Other variables affect accurate measurement of rainfall. But the most important problem is wind. Ground-level gauges will collect more rain, and tend to be more accurate, than those above ground, especially if accompanied by an antisplash grid. If the rain gauge is set above the ground, high winds can create uneven distribution of rain and splashing of water onto, rather than into, the gauge.

The problems in measuring rainfall are minor compared to measuring snowfall. Wind is a particular problem since blowing snow, rather than falling snow, might accumulate in gauges, particularly ground-level gauges. The temperature when the snow was formed, wind patterns, and how long the snow has been caught in the gauge may determine whether snow accumulates in air-filled, feathery layers or is compacted down to a tight, dense pack. Since the density of fallen snow varies tremendously, scientists require some way to compare snowfalls accumulated under different conditions.

Meteorologists use several techniques to deal with these problems:

1. Snow boards. These boards are put out on the ground. The accumulation is measured on an hourly basis and then cleaned off. This labor-intensive method assures a reading before the snow can pack down. But any one board might not be representative of an area, so many must be used if an accurate assessment of precipitation is important.

2. Weighing. Essentially the same technique we discussed with rain gauges. A heating element is put into a gauge (often a standard rain gauge) so that the snow melts. The water is then weighed and converted into "inches."

3. Snow pillows. These immediately record the weight of the snow that accumulates above them without converting the snow into water.

Submitted by Ted Roter of Los Angeles, California. Thanks also to Valerie M. Shields of Danville, California.

What Does the "FD&C" Found on Food and Shampoo Labels Mean?

The "FD&C" on the label assures that the dyes used in the product have the stamp of approval of the U.S. government. Although since nobody seems to know what in the heck "FD&C" means, it's not clear how much assurance is really provided.

The letters stand for Food, Drug, [and] Cosmetic. In 1938, the Food, Drug, and Cosmetic Act gave the FDA the authority to regulate the dyes used in these three categories of products. At the present time, seven dyes may be used in all three; 26 dyes are approved for drugs and cosmetics only; and two "Ext." dyes ("D" and "C") are approved for drugs or cosmetics designed for external use only (e.g., a skin lotion) and not subject to accidental or incidental ingestion (e.g., lipstick).

Submitted by Patrick Chambers of Grandview, Missouri.

How Can Fingernails and Hair Grow After Someone Dies?

They can't. But that doesn't stop this ancient myth from persisting.

We'll give you the real story. But don't read this while eating, please. And remember, this Imponderable wasn't our idea. We just pursue truth anywhere we find it.

The tissues of a corpse dry out rather quickly. As the skin dries out, it shrinks, but hair and nails don't break down as quickly as the surrounding skin. If the same quantity of hair, for example, surrounds a partially shrunken/evaporated skull, the hair will apppear to have grown.

We once spoke to a funeral director who honestly believed that men's beards grew after they died. Why else, he asked, would we sometimes have to shave them more than once before the funeral? The answer, of course, is that the hair didn't grow, but the stubble that might have been obscured at the time of death now showed through after the surrounding skin had shrunk.

The "nail illusion" is heightened because the skin around the fingers and toes tends to dry out particularly quickly, just as it is the first to wrinkle and expand when wet (a phenomenon we discussed in *Why Do Clocks Run Clockwise?*).

Not all corpses dry out in this way. If a corpse is kept in a moist place, it can develop adipocere, a fatty, waxy substance. Corpses with adipocere do not tend to display the hair or nail illusion.

Submitted by Loretta McDonough of Frontenac, Missouri, who is probably sorry she ever asked.

What Is the Purpose of the White Dot on the Frog of a Violin Bow?

For those unfamiliar with the term, the frog of a bow (used for any string instrument) is the screw that secures the hair of the bow and keeps it away from the stick at the point where the player holds the bow. In England, the frog is called the "nut";

the frog serves much the same purpose as a nut in American hardware terminology. While the frog is now adjustable so that the tension of the bow hair can be modified, it was originally fixed.

Although the frog serves a vital function, the sole purpose of the white dot is to look pretty. In fact, one lover of music once carried this decorative function to extremes. Alvin Johnson, of the American Musicological Society, related the following story about one of our titans of industry.

Henry Ford was an eccentric man and rich enough to indulge his idiosyncrasies. Ford loved square dancing and used to invite a string quartet of quite exalted fiddlers from his local symphony orchestra to play for him in his mansion. Ford and his dance partners were listening to square dancing played on four Stradivari violins. Ford insisted on putting in a diamond to decorate the frog of each bow.

Submitted By Garland Lyn of Windsor, Connecticut.

Why Does Traffic on Highways Tend to Clump Together in Bunches?

Four factors conspire to create clumps:

1. Moderately heavy or heavy volume of traffic.
2. Uneven speeds of vehicles.
3. The unwillingness of slow vehicles to move to the right-hand lane(s).
4. Uneven flow of traffic onto the highway.

Most clumps are caused when fast drivers pull up to slower-moving vehicles and can't get around them to pass. On an empty highway, one car can't block faster cars from passing. But on an already crowded highway, a relatively slow-moving car is as likely to be found in the left lane as the right lane. Alongside other vehicles traveling at approximately the same speed, they form a shield as impermeable as the defensive line of the Chicago Bears.

Richard Cunard, engineer of traffic and operations at the Transportation Research Board, told *Imponderables* that uneven traffic flow onto freeways from onramps can also cause clumps to form. When a green light on a major access road allows scores of cars to enter a highway at the same time, the slow-moving vehicles traveling in the right-hand lane scamper to the left to avoid slowing down to accommodate the newcomers. Fast-moving cars in the left-hand lanes then try to find faster hunting ground to their left. The result: a chain reaction in which all vehicles try to avoid the worst possible eventuality, an American tragedy—traveling at a slower rate than they would wish.

In an attempt to counteract the effect of inflowing traffic upon congestion and clumping, some cities have installed traffic lights on their onramps that restrict traffic flow onto freeways. The more sophisticated systems contain sensing devices that monitor the traffic in the right-hand lane of the freeway. Only when there are openings in the right-hand lanes do the sensing devices "tell" the signal at the onramp to turn green.

Clumps form just as easily on an interstate with two lanes in each direction as on urban freeways. On a two-lane road with even moderately heavy traffic, a few slow drivers who refuse to pull over to the right are sufficient to create clumps that can cause traffic jams for miles behind. Of course, these interstate highways carry signs that say "Slow Traffic—Keep Right.

But what is "slow traffic"? Is a driver traveling at the speed limit a slowpoke? Must you pull over everytime a joy rider going 80 miles per hour bears down on you? If you prize your rear bumper, the answer is yes. And yielding to the speed demon on your tail also accomplishes the task of helping to eradicate the scourge of clumping.

Submitted by John Benson of Auburn, California.

Why Do Home Doors Open Inward While Doors in Public Buildings Open Outward?

Interviewers sometimes ask us what percentage of the folks who pose an Imponderable also supply the answer. Our reply: fewer than one percent.

Many times, readers have given us leads or provided incorrect information. Good Imponderables are harder to find than answers anyway, and it takes us just as long to verify a theory proposed by a reader as it does to do original research.

But we're proud to announce that this Imponderable is a one-percenter. Dorothea McGee posed this Imponderable and after consulting with several architects, we know that her answer below was right too.

> Public buildings are obliged to have "panic bars" that open the door outward in case of fire or emergency. If a crowd is pushing to get out, the mob does not have to be backed away from the door to get out. Such doors are very expensive and have concealed hinges.
>
> At home, if confronted with an emergency, you are not faced with a large crowd pushing at once. Even in case of fire, you could get the family to move back enough to open the door.
>
> But in order to get large pieces of furniture into the house, you want easily removed doors. Since all you have to do is knock out the pin to take the door down, the pin has to be inside, where burglars can't reach. Also, you can put up a storm door without having the two doors bang into each other.

Architects have assured me that there are ways to install storm doors with outward-opening doors and that skilled burglars can get furniture out of just about any house they want, but the convenience of the outward-opening door for residences is clear. Architect Bill Stanley notes that at one time residential doors were barred from within to prevent intruders from pulling them open.

Submitted by Dorothea McGee of Paterson, New Jersey.

When Glass Breaks, Why Don't the Pieces Fit Back Together Perfectly?

We received a wonderful response to this Imponderable from Harold Blake, who you might remember from *When Do Fish Sleep?* as the gentleman who spent some time in college simulating the aroma of Juicy Fruit gum. It's nice to know that Mr. Blake, now a retired engineer, is still trying to find the solutions to the important things in life.

They key point Blake makes about this Imponderable is to remember that while glass appears to be inflexible, it does bend and change shape. If you throw a ball through a plate glass window, the glass will try to accommodate the force thrust upon it; it will bend. But if bent beyond its limits, glass shatters or ruptures.

At the point that the glass breaks, the glass's shape is distorted but the break is a perfect fracture—the parts would fit back together again. But as soon as the glass shatters, the parts begin to minimize their distortion and return to the unstressed state.

When the pieces return to their unstressed state, the fracture is no longer "perfect." Like a human relationship, things are never quite the same after a breakup.

Blake points out that other seemingly inflexible materials show the same tendencies as glass. Ceramics, pottery, and metals, for example, also distort and then return to a slightly altered "original" configuration.

Submitted by Charles Venezia of Iselin, New Jersey.

Guess who brushed with ...

expiro•DENT Toothpaste

We don't need a "use by" date—it's BAD now!

Why Is There No Expiration Date on Toothpaste? Does Toothpaste Ever "Go Bad"?

After we received this Imponderable from a caller on a radio talk show, we were reminded of a personal experience. We once found large tubes of Colgate toothpaste on sale at a discount store for 49 cents apiece. Not ones to pass up a gift horse, we bought a couple of tubes only to discover, when we brought them home, that the toothpaste was manufactured in Venezuela. All the writing on the packaging was in Spanish.

We worried about exactly how old the toothpaste was. So we dumped the toothpaste in the cabinet under our bathroom sink and didn't think about it for a couple of years until one day we had run out of toothpaste. Searching for a fresh tube, we encountered one of the old Spanish language tubes? Was it safe to use?

No sign of an expiration date could be found on the tube. We opened the cap. It smelled okay. We had a social commitment that night and mulled over the alternatives. What was more important, our health or fresh breath?

So, of course, we brushed our teeth with the aged toothpaste. And we lived.

Many foods and all drugs are normally marked with an expiration date. But toothpaste isn't quite a drug and isn't quite a food. What is it? With luck, an effective decay preventive dentifrice, of course!

Both Colgate and Crest informed us that toothpaste has no expiration date. The flavor might change slightly over the years (although the Colgate didn't), but it remains effective as a cavity fighter.

Procter & Gamble was kind enough to send a list of the ingredients in Crest toothpaste; as you will see, there is nothing in the paste that seems perishable (or appetizing):

Ingredient	Function
Sodium Fluoride	The active ingredient; protects the teeth against cavities.
Hydrated Silica	The abrasive of Crest; polishes and cleans the teeth.
Sorbitol and/or Glycerin	Prevents paste from hardening and keeps Crest smooth and creamy.
Trisodium Phosphate & Sodium Phosphate	These buffers keep Crest at a neutral pH of 7.
Sodium lauryl sulfate	Foaming agent; penetrates and loosens deposits on tooth surface.
Titanium Dioxide	Makes toothpaste opaque.
Xanthan Gum & Carbomer-940 or Carbomer-956	These hold the toothpaste together.
Sodium Saccharin	Sweetener
FD&C Blue #1	Colorant
Regular Flavor	Imparts a wintergreen taste.
Mint Flavor	Imparts a spearmint taste.
Gel Flavor	Imparts a sweet spice taste.
Water	The medium into which the ingredients are dissolved.
Mica (Crest for kids only)	Sparkles

Why Do Apples and Pears Discolor So Quickly When Peeled?

Our theory about this Imponderable is simple. We have had it drummed into our heads by teachers, parents, and nutritionists that the peels of fruits are the "best" part for us, full of vitamins and fiber. The spotting of fruits is nature's way of forcing the point—who is going to peel an apple when one is stuck with leopard-skin flesh?

But pomologists (who study fruits, not hands) insist on a more technical explanation. The discoloration in fruits, including peaches, apricots, and bananas, as well as apples and pears, is caused by oxidation. The catalyst for the oxidation is an enzyme, polyphenol oxidase.

According to John B. Williams, of California Apple Products, Inc., polyphenol oxidase occurs naturally in all sugar-producing fruits in varying amounts: "The amount of this enzyme will determine how quickly the browning occurs. The peel of most fruits will not allow oxygen to penetrate in sufficient quantities to act as a catalyst for the enzyme." Banana peels are more porous than apple or pear skins, allowing oxygen to penetrate into the fruit while the skin is still in place. The sturdier apple peel is unlikely to discolor unless it is bruised or cut open.

Submitted by Launi Rountry of Brockton, Massachusetts.
Thanks also to Debby Birli of Richmond Heights, Ohio.

Why Do You Usually See Revolving Doors Only in Big Cities?

The main purpose of revolving doors, according to Mike Fisher, vice-president of sales and marketing for door manufacturer

Besam Inc., is to help preserve conditioned air (heat in winter and air conditioning in the summer), thus saving money on energy bills. The constant opening and closing of conventional doors plays havoc with temperature regulation.

Most tall buildings, of course, are found in big cities and almost any skyscraper is going to have revolving doors. Why? The taller a building is, the more "stack pressure" is exerted, forcing hot air to rise more than it normally would during cold weather. Stack pressure creates the wind tunnel effect you often find on the ground floor of skyscrapers.

Revolving doors are not cheap. The lowliest model might cost $8,000 or $10,000, while the revolving doors at Trump Plaza cost more than $100,000 apiece. In order to justify the price of a revolving door, owners want to see tangible savings in their energy bills.

Fisher argues that revolving doors can quickly become cost-efficient. The Newark airport recently installed revolving doors in a terminal's entrance and found that the cost of the doors was paid back in only three years.

Ray Sowers, of Tubelite, adds that revolving doors also lend a patina of prestige to a building, and that not all purchases can be attributed to cold-blooded, bottom-line considerations. Sowers has noticed that if his company has installed a revolving door in a building, Tubelite often gets an order from a building across the street. The revolving door is a bit of a status symbol.

Several of our sources mentioned that it was difficult to convince many architects in the warmer climes to install revolving doors, for they do not seem as concerned about losing air conditioning in the summer as they are about losing heat in winter, even though the energy loss can be just as expensive and uncomfortable. But this explains why revolving doors are comparatively scarce in even large cities in the South and West.

The day of revolving doors in small cities and even small towns might be at hand. Fisher is particularly excited about two comparatively new applications of automatic revolving doors. In airports, they are prized for their security advantages in directing traffic flow in one direction. And there is a real chance that many supermarkets might install automatic revolving doors. D'Agostino, a chain in New York City, has recently installed them in several of their stores, in order to better regulate both the conditioned air in the stores and, most importantly from an economic standpoint, the fragile temperature control of their refrigerated cases. If the door manufacturers can convince Kroger and A&P that it is cost-efficient to install automatic revolving doors, the premise of this Imponderable will soon be obsolete.

Submitted by Rosemary Mangano of Flushing, New York and E.A. Hammerschmidt of Casper, Wyoming.

Why Are You Instructed to Put Cold Water into an Automatic Drip Coffeemaker?

Since coffeemakers eventually heat water to 190–200 degrees Fahrenheit, hotter than the hot water out of a tap, we never understood why it made a difference what temperature water is put into the coffeemaker. All of the coffee experts we contacted concurred: The only reason you need to put cold water into a coffeemaker is because the brewed coffee will taste better.

Hot water has a tendency to taste flat and stale. Hot water pipes tend to be corroded, contributing off-tastes to the water. Cold water tends to be full of oxygen and desirable minerals, yielding a more flavorful cup of coffee.

The rule of thumb in the coffee industry is that you shouldn't put water into a coffeemaker that you wouldn't want to drink straight. According to the National Coffee Association of U.S.A., zeolite-type softened water is a particular failure when used to brew coffee.

Submitted by Reverend Dale Huelsman of Wellington, Ohio.

What Accounts for the Great Difference in Climate between the Atlantic Coast and Pacific Coast of the U.S.?

If you are like us, you glaze over during weathercasts on the local news. The intricacies of the weather map, complete with air flows and troughs, strike us as no easier to comprehend than quantum physics. Why waste five valuable minutes on a weather report when all we want to know is whether we need an umbrella or an overcoat? After all, the four minutes saved could be devoted to more important news, like a graphic depiction of another grisly murder or a juicy political scandal.

"It Never Rains in Southern California," warbled Albert Hammond in his 1972 gold record. Not quite accurate, Albert, but not a bad meteorological generalization from someone who spent most of his life in Gibraltar. The weather is more moderate on the left coast and certainly much warmer in winter. Why is this?

The one principle we have managed to glean from those weathercasts is that the prevailing winds in North America move from west to east. We inherit the weather from the west of us. The sea is much slower to change in climate and temperature than land masses. Although the Pacific Ocean has its share of storms, they are relatively infrequent and are usually associated with moderate weather. So the West Coast receives relatively infrequent storms and moderate weather.

Sol Hirsch, executive director of the National Weather Association, told *Imponderables* that the Rocky Mountains are most responsible for the colder and stormier weather of the east coast (and the Midwest, for that matter):

> The weather in the east is determined by storm systems developing from the Rockies eastward that are generally moving in easterly or northerly directions, due to the rotation of the earth. In addition, the area east of the Rockies is exposed to cold air coming from Canada whereas cold air west of the Rockies is infrequent.

The collision of multiple fronts east of the Rockies manufactures storms and makes the weather patterns volatile and difficult to predict.

Of course, the volatility of weather in the East makes the job of a weathercaster considerably dicier than his West Coast counterpart's. If a weathercaster in southern California predicts "85 degrees and partly cloudy" during the summer and "75 degrees and partly cloudy" during the other three seasons, he won't be too far wrong.

Why Do Some Oranges Have an Extra Wedge of Fruit?

You won't find that extra piece of fruit on most oranges. The technical name for the extra piece is the "secondary fruit," and along with its seedlessness and visible navel, it is one of the genetic characteristics of the navel orange.

Catherine A. Clay, an information specialist for the Florida Department of Citrus, told *Imponderables* how the wedge develops:

> All citrus fruit starts out as a blossom on the tree. Each blossom has two sets of ovaries. With many varieties of citrus, the fruit grows around only the primary ovaries and excludes the secondary ovaries. However, with the navel variety and some mandarin oranges such as tangerines, the fruit grows over both sets of ovaries. The cone-shaped section, or secondary fruit, within the navel is actually an undeveloped "twin" of the primary fruit. The secondary fruit will never become a fully developed fruit.

Secondary fruits can be found in some varieties of grapefruits, temple oranges, and tangelos.

Navel oranges grown in humid, subtropical climates, such as Florida, the Caribbean, and parts of South America, tend to have larger navels and secondary fruit than those produced in drier climates with cool winters (e.g., California, South Australia, and Israel). The larger opening of the Florida navel causes problems with cultivation of the crop, for it provides a convenient nesting area for insects, mites, and fungi. Although the pests may enter through the small fruitlet, they can penetrate and eventually contaminate the primary fruit.

Submitted by Jim Sears of Belton, Missouri.

HOW Do the Trick Birthday Candles (That Keep Relighting after Being Blown Out) Work?

Michael DeMent, Product Spokesperson for Hallmark, told us that the wicks of their Puff Proof® Candles are treated with magnesium crystals. The crystals retain enough heat to reilluminate the wick after candles are blown out.

Because the magnesium-treated wicks retain heat so well, Hallmark recommends extinguishing the candles permanently by dipping them in water.

DeMent shocked us (and in this job, we're not easily shocked) by telling us that practical jokers aren't the only customers for trick birthday candles. Some penurious types view them not as trick candles but as *reusable* candles. After the candles are blown out for the first time, they gather the candles and pinch the wicks with their hands or surround them with a paper towel or other material so that the heat is allowed to radiate around the other object. They then rebox the candles and use them another time.

Not only is the birthday boy or girl deprived of a little fun, but my guess is that the honoree isn't going to get a Porsche or a VCR as a gift from such a cheapskate.

Submitted by Angel Rivera and Dodde Stark of Atlantic Highlands, New Jersey.

Why Doesn't Honey Spoil?

How many foods can you think of that don't spoil AND don't have a long ingredient list full of words with four or more syllables on their labels? Bees may be nasty little insects, but they sure know how to produce a durable product.

By far the most important reason honey doesn't spoil is its high acid content. Ordinary yeasts and bacteria simply can't survive in the acidic environment.

According to Dr. Richard Nowogrodzki, of the Office of Apiculture at Cornell University, honey has a very high osmotic pressure, which means that foreign microorganisms that enter honey rapidly lose water. Yeasts literally dehydrate and die. Nowogrodzki adds that one group of fungi, the osmophilic yeasts, can survive in honey but cannot grow to cause spoilage unless the water content increases to levels above those usually found in stored honey.

In order to protect the honey even when the moisture level increases, bees also add an enzyme (glucose oxidase) to the nectar when they are transforming it into honey. Nowogrodzki explains:

> This enzyme is inactive in honey unless the honey becomes diluted; in diluted honey the enzyme catalyzes a reaction that turns some of the glucose into glutonic acid (thereby further increasing the acidity of the honey) and hydrogen peroxide, which is a common household disinfectant that kills bacteria and fungi (including osmophilic yeasts).

Spoilage of honey is actually the result of fermentation. When the sugar-tolerant yeasts act upon the sugars in honey, alcohol and carbon dioxide is created. Spoilage is most likely to occur after honey has granulated, because the liquid remaining in the nongranulated honey contains too much water. Since honey yeasts will not grow below about 52 degrees Fahrenheit, storing honey in temperatures of 50 degrees or lower is a safe way to prevent granulation.

Scientists have long known that by simply keeping the water level of honey below 17 percent and/or by heating the honey to 145 degrees for about a half-hour, fermentation can be prevented.

Submitted by Douglas Watkins, Jr. of Hayward, California.
Thanks also to Robert M. Chamberlin of Rochester, Minnesota,
and Cary L. Chapman of Homeland, California.

HOW Did the "Grandfather" Clock Get Its Name?

Dutch astronomer Christian Huygens created the weight and pendulum clock in the mid-seventeenth century. He died long before his invention was dubbed the "grandfather clock."

Two hundred years later, in the United States, Pennsylvania German settlers considered the weight and pendulum clock (often called a long-case clock) a status symbol akin to the BMW or satellite dish of today. The popularity of floor clocks soon spread throughout the country.

But the name shift began in 1876, when popular Connecticut songwriter Henry Clay Work produced his masterpiece, "My Grandfather's Clock," which contained the immortal lyrics:

> My grandfather's clock was too long for the shelf,
> So it stood ninety years on the floor.

Clock owners shrugged off the sarcastic tone of Clay's song and adopted "grandfather" proudly, marking a rare case when a 200-year-old technology was renamed.

Submitted by Alex Soto of Potsdam, New York.

What Happens to the Little Punchings That Are Created by the Perforations in Postage Stamps?

Our correspondent adds that he worked for the postal system for 32 years, retired in 1979, and could never get an answer to this question. We're happy to report that we have found the answer. Now you can enjoy your retirement in peace.

Peter G. Papadopoulos, philatelic programs analyst at the Stamp Administration and Advisory Branch of the United States Postal Service (try to fit that title on a postage stamp!), told us that these hole punchings are called "chad." Environmentalists won't be too happy about the fate of chad: "They are sucked up by a vacuum during the perforation process and destroyed with other scrap paper."

Submitted by J. J. Feuhrer of San Diego, California. Thanks also to Dwight Siemens of Clovis, California.

Why Do We Carve Jack-o'-Lanterns on Halloween?

The modern celebration of Halloween has ancient and paradoxical roots. All Hallow's Day (also known as All Saint's Day) was proclaimed by Pope Gregory III in the eighth century. The new holiday was created for a practical reason: The Church had more martyrs and saints to honor than there were days of the week.

But long before the Christian celebration took hold, Druids had observed October 31 as Sambain ("summer's end"), the end of the Celtic year, a celebration of the summer's harvest, and an appeasement to the sun god and the god of the dead. The Druids believed that the souls of everyone who died in the last year dwelled in the bodies of animals. Only on October 31 would their souls reappear to visit their relatives.

Unfortunately, these revisits weren't congenial family reunions. Rather, the dead were thought to come back as witches, ghosts, and hobgoblins, and to wreak havoc across the land. The tradition of lighting bonfires on Halloween stems from the Druids' belief that the fires would frighten away evil spirits.

As Christian belief overcame pagan superstition in Ireland and Scotland, celebrants took over the role of mischief makers from supernatural apparitions. In the early United States, Halloween was not a big deal. Early settlers were mostly Protestants who didn't observe All Saint's Day back in Europe. But with the Irish immigration of the 1840s, America received citizens steeped not only in Catholic educations but with remnants of some of the Druid practices of Sambain.

One of the oldest Sambain traditions was for celebrants to carry a jack-o'-lantern. In Scotland, turnips were used; in Ireland, large potatoes and rutabagas were popular. But in the United States, pumpkins were much more abundant. The jack-o'-lantern was carried all during the night, not left on a windowsill as a sitting duck for roving kids. The scary faces carved on the pumpkins were presumably there to replicate the goblins and evil spirits once believed to rule on Sambain.

Why is the lantern called Jack? Nobody really knows for sure, although Irish legend claims that the Devil once came to claim the soul of a no-good man named Jack. But Jack outsmarted the Devil several times and stayed alive. When Jack eventually died, neither heaven nor hell would claim Jack.

Consigned to an afterlife without a home, Jack begged the Devil for a live coal to provide light so he could navigate in limbo. The Devil, who, as always, was a soft touch when it came to Jack, gave him a piece. Jack put the coal into a turnip. And Jack is still walking around with his lantern until either heaven or hell will open its door to him.

Submitted by Debby Birli of Richmond Heights, Ohio. Thanks also to John Bova of Cheektowaga, New York.

What's the Difference Between a Fast and a Slow Busy Signal on the Telephone?

According to Shelly Gilbreath and Ray Bombardieri, of Southwestern Bell Telephone, a fast busy signal, most often heard when trying to place a long-distance call, indicates that there isn't enough equipment available to process your call:

> The fast busy signal signifies that all trunks either receiving originating call signals, or all the trunks to the terminating end, are engaged and are at a capacity load. If the originating caller were to hang up and try again within a few moments, the call would most likely go through.
>
> Whether or not the party on the receiving end is engaged on the phone has no bearing on if you hear a fast busy signal.

The fast busy signal, a nonverbal variation of the prerecorded message "all circuits are busy," signals 120 times per minute, compared to the less feverish pace of the "regular" busy signal, which sounds 60 times per minute. Of course, the slow busy signal simply indicates that the person on the other end of the phone has found someone more interesting to talk to at the moment than you.

Submitted by Mike Luxton of Long Beach, California.

Where Does the Wax Go in Dripless Candles?

Into the flame itself. There are 67 different grades of paraffin, ranging from extremely soft (with low-temperature melting points) to extremely hard (with high-temperature melting points). Conventional candles use candles with such low melting points that most will melt in the sun.

Dripless candles use hard paraffin and longer wicks, so that no wax is in direct contact with the flame and so the wax around the wick won't melt or drip.

Submitted by Chuck and Louisa Keighan of Portland, Oregon. Thanks also to Stephen J. Michalak of Myrtle Beach, South Carolina; Mike Hutson of Visalia, California; Richard Roberts of Memphis, Tennessee; and Beth Kennedy of Exeter, New Hampshire.

HOW Did the Heights of Light Switches Become Established? Why Are They Located a Foot Above the Door Knob?

William J. Stanley, a member emeritus of the American Institute of Architects, is much amused by this Imponderable. He agrees that it would make much more sense to place light switches on the wall adjacent to the door knob, so that they could be reached more easily in the dark. But there is a reason for our illogical height standards:

> If you ask a real estate salesman about this he will probably claim that the purpose is to keep the switch out of the reach of small children. But this is not the real reason.
>
> Nearly all houses have the electrical distribution lines in the "attic" or ceiling joist space, from which individual circuits are dropped down inside the wall cavity. But some building codes require that the space between wall studs must be fire-blocked at or near midheight. The light switch boxes are placed just above the fire blocking to save the cost of making a hole through the blocking for the wire.

Stanley adds that many modern versions of building codes now allow the blocking to be lowered (or in some cases, eliminated altogether), allowing:

... the switches to be placed opposite the door knobs where they belong. The small amount of extra wire that this would require does not seem like a sufficient reason to perpetuate this anachronism. Of course, you may still have trouble getting an electrician or builder to admit that they are just cutting corners, based on an old rule that people had become accustomed to!

We wondered whether the height standards for light switches were standard throughout the world. They aren't. New York architect Nick Fusco, who has spent time in Japan, reports that not only the light switches but the door frames of Japanese residences are placed lower than their Western counterparts. Tourists might not notice the difference because many hotels built to cater to foreigners are built to a "higher" standard.

Submitted by John Clark of Pittsburgh, Pennsylvania.

Why Does the Difference between 75 Degrees and 80 Degrees in Water Temperature Feel Quite Severe When a Five-Degree Difference in the Ambient Air Barely Registers?

The conductivity of water is much higher than air. If the water in a swimming pool is colder than body temperature, the water will conduct heat quickly away from our bodies. If it is warmer, such as in a hot tub, the water just as rapidly transfers heat to the body. Difference in temperature in the ambient air transfer heat in the same directions but at a much slower rate.

Richard A. Anthes, president of the University Corporation for Atmospheric Research, emphasized to *Imponderables:* "It is the rate of conduction of heat that we sense as heat or cold."

Submitted by Glenn Worthman of Palo Alto, California.

SORRY, BUT OUR MIRROR IS STUCK ON THE "NIGHT" POSITION !!!

What Happens When You Flip the Day/Night Switch on the Rear-View Mirror of an Automobile? Why Do You See Only Lights When the Mirror is in the "Night" Position?

The best explanation we found for this Imponderable was supplied by Thomas J. Carr, director of safety and international technical affairs for the Motor Vehicle Manufacturers Association of the United States, which represents Chrysler, Ford, General Motors, Honda of America, Navistar International, Paccar, and Volvo North America. Carr disillusioned us about the reflective qualities of glass, but then solving Imponderables often involves disabusing ourselves of the innocence of youth:

> With a day/night mirror in the day position, the image is "seen" on the reflective coating that covers the back of the glass. In effect, the visual image passes through the glass to the highly efficient reflective coating and then back out to the viewer. About 80 percent of the incident (incoming) light is reflected with the mirror in the "day" position.

When the mirror is in the "night" position, the reflective coating that was used in the "day" position is tilted away so that the front surface of the mirror glass becomes the reflector. Because glass is a much less efficient reflector, only about 4 percent of the incident light actually reaches the viewer's eyes. Because so much less of the light is transmitted in this position, most of the background that provides reference cues to place a following vehicle in the scene is lost. You only see the lights of the vehicle and perhaps its outline.

Submitted by Kevin A. Shaw of Cincinnati, Ohio. Thanks also to Susan Irias of River Ridge, Louisiana, and Michelle Madsen of McMinnville, Oregon.

What Vegetables Are Used in Vegetable Oils?

If a company is selling 100% corn, peanut, or safflower oil, it will trumpet the identity of the vegetable in marquee-sized letters on the label. So it is natural that most consumers, when faced with the words "vegetable oil" on a label, assume that the contents consist of either a "bad" oil, such as the cottonseed, coconut, or palm oil that cardiologists are constantly warning us about, or a blend of several different vegetables.

In fact, until recently, many vegetable oils were blends. But now all the major brands, such as Wesson and Crisco, as well as most generic or store-brand vegetable oils, use 100% soybean oil in their "vegetable oil."

Although soybean oil has most of the characteristics of the "good" oils, the North American consumer hasn't yet embraced soybeans but will pay a premium for corn oil or peanut oil. Until consumers are convinced that soybeans are more desirable than "vegetable oil," soybeans will continue to forego star billing on the label and appear only in the fine print.

Submitted by Muriel S. Marschke of Katonah, New York.

Why Do Toilets in Public Restrooms Make an Explosive Noise When Flushed?

Perhaps this isn't the most uplifting Imponderable of all time, but we're not judgmental types. If you wonder about a question, even a bathroom Imponderable, it's our job to, well, eliminate it.

The biggest difference between home and public toilets is that most home units work on gravity. But toilets in public restrooms utilize line pressure (created by turning the flush valve) so that the water pressure is much greater than a gravity-driven toilet.

Increasing the line pressure does not use any more water per flush. So managers and owners of big buildings are willing to put up with the sonic booms in exchange for the assurance that "customers" won't have to flush more than once.

We spoke to Jim Datka, of giant American Standard, which makes toilets for homes and institutions. He added that a couple of other factors exacerbate the "explosion" made in public restrooms. The acoustics in most public bathrooms couldn't be better for magnifying and echoing sounds: ceramic tiles; metal stalls; and not a shred of fabric to absorb the noise. Also, the metal flush valve is left exposed in the public restroom, instead of being obscured in a china tank, which helps swallow the cacophony in your home.

One more Imponderable down the drain.

Submitted by Mike, a caller on the Ray Briem show, KABC-AM, Los Angeles, California.

Why Is the Bottom of One- and Two-Liter Cola Bottles Black? Is the Black Bottom Piece There for Functional or Aesthetic Reasons?

The "base cup" is very much a practical and integral part of a bottle. M. Claire Jackson, of Coca-Cola USA, explains:

> The polyethylene terephthalate bottles are manufactured in a two-step process. They are first injection molded into a "preform" that looks like a test tube threaded at one end. The preform is then reheated and "blow-molded" into its final shape and size.

Because the bottoms of most plastic bottles are rounded, they will not stand upright without the base cup.

Why are the base cups black? In most cases, the black cup signifies that the bottle contains a dark beverage, such as a cola or root beer. Most lemon-lime and ginger ale bottles have green bases. Many companies that market flavored seltzers color-code their base cups (e.g., red for raspberry flavored, yellow for lemon, orange for mandarin orange), making it much easier to select your favorite flavor from crowded aisles of the supermarket.

Because it is a neutral color, black has become the "default" color for base cups. Margie A. Spurlock, manager of consumer affairs for Royal Crown Cola Co., told *Imponderables* that black tends to be visually compatible with the colors of most trademarked logos. And economics might enter the picture: "Some bottlers buy bare plastic bottles and label them as they are filled. Basic black affords them the option of buying in larger quantities for a better price."

Submitted by Marguerite McLeod of Braintree, Massachusetts.

Where Does the Sound of a Telephone Ring Emanate From? Why Does the First Ring Sometimes Start in the Middle While Other First Rings Go On as Long as Subsequent Rings? Why Do Receiving Parties Sometimes Pick up the Phone before the Caller Hears a Ring? Why Do Some American Phones and Many Foreign Phones Ring Twice in Succession?

The answer to all four of these Imponderables lies in the circuitry of the switches (also known as "central offices") of local phone companies. The ringing signal comes from the switches, not your telephone.

Ever notice how regular and rhythmic a phone ring is? That's because the ringing signal is precise and symmetrical—a constant cycle of four seconds of silence alternating with two seconds of ringing. When you dial the first three digits of a local number on a touch-tone phone, the sophisticated routing system is already directing your call to the appropriate switch in the receiver's area. By the time you punch in the last four digits, the switch quickly triggers the ringing mechanism on the receiver's line, and that same switch closest to the receiver's end trips a signal to start a ring on your phone.

But the ring signals to the caller and the receiver are not always precisely synchronized. If the circuits are overloaded, the switch that sends a signal to the receiver may be incapable of sending the same message back to the caller at that instant. If so, another switch is tripped and the caller's ring cycle will be different from the receiver's.

Because the ringing cycle is silent twice as long as it generates noise, the caller and receiver are exactly twice as likely to hear a full ring as a shortened one. So when the receiving party picks up the phone immediately upon hearing the phone ring, there is a chance he picked up before the caller heard a ring (when the caller was at the end of the four-second silent phase of the cycle). The next time this happens, compliment the receiver on his or her quick reflexes, and don't assume you have just undergone a paranormal experience.

Double-ring phones used to be much more common. Dick Hofacker, of AT&T Bell Laboratories, told us that multirings used to signal party-line users which particular customer was being favored by a call. PBX systems sometimes used multiring signals to indicate whether a call was coming from an in-house or external party. Local phone companies can set their switching equipment to execute single or double ringing codes; the switches at the receiver's end determine what kind of ring both parties hear. Nobody we spoke to could explain why many European countries favor double rings. Until recently, our esteemed publisher, HarperCollins, favored them. All we know is that it is rather easy, as Shelly Gilbreath, of Southwestern Bell Telephone explained, to set the codes to be "spaced differently, with short or long and/or fast or slow pulses."

Submitted by Mark Carroll of Nashville, Tennessee. Thanks also to Henry J. Stark of Montgomery, New York; Jon R. Kennedy of Charlotte, North Carolina; and Dr. Fred Feldman of Pacific Palisades, California.

Why Don't Barefoot Field Goal Kickers and Punters Get Broken Feet?

Jeff Atkinson, a former National Football League kicker, told *Imponderables* that most kickers detest the drag of a shoe, for the faster a kicker can get his foot through the ball, the farther he can kick it. Although most football kickers favor sleek, tight-fitting soccer shoes, a minority favor kicking in the buff. The thought is enough to make you cringe.

But barefoot kickers don't break their feet. Why not? In the now omnipresent soccer-style field goal kick, the foot meets the ball not on the toes but well above them, where the laces of the shoe would be if they were wearing shoes, and a little to the left of center (for right-footed kickers). Sports physician John R. McCarroll adds that if the kick is properly executed, the ball is struck by a flat surface of the most stable parts of the foot.

Why are there fewer barefoot punters than place-kickers? Because punts are executed on the outside rather than the inside of the foot. If you kick a punt on the same spot as a place-kick, the ball won't spiral properly. The outside of the foot is a little more susceptible to pain and injury than the inside of the foot, so there are fewer barefoot punters.

Atkinson says that the one time barefoot kickers often regret their choice is when kicking off. The most pain a kicker is likely to sustain is not from the football but from the hard plastic that holds the ball, which players sometimes hit accidentally.

Submitted by Dr. Roger Alexander of San Diego, California.

Why Is the Hot Water Faucet on the Left and the Cold Water Faucet on the Right?

This earth-shattering question is undoubtedly one of our ten most often asked Imponderables. But it has another distinction. This is the first Imponderable we have ever resuscitated from the dead-Imponderables file.

All of our usual plumbing experts struck out when faced with this Imponderable. "Tradition," they would say. "The cold water faucet has to be on one side or the other, doesn't it?" commented the less patient. Despairing of ever getting an answer, we expunged this Imponderable from our rolls and assumed that the answer would be lost in antiquity forever.

Then one night, on the Ray Briem Show in Los Angeles, a caller asked this Imponderable for the eight-millionth time and we verbally shrugged our shoulders. But then a plumber from a rural area called and expressed disbelief that we didn't know the answer. Here is a summary of what he said:

> You young whippersnappers. Don't you remember when there wasn't such a thing as a hot water faucet? Cold-water-only faucets placed the knob or lever on the right. Why not? Most people are right-handed. When hot water plumbing was introduced, it made sense to keep the cold water on the right and place the hot water on the left.

Makes sense to us. The anonymous plumber added that he still encounters a few cold-water-only sinks on his job. The knob or lever is always on the right.

We called our trusty old plumbing experts to verify the plumber's tale and they admitted that his explanation made sense to them. But since they haven't manufactured cold-water-only faucets for many a moon, we can't prove that this answer is the full explanation.

Submitted by Josh Gibson of Silver Spring, Maryland. Thanks also to Kyle Tolle of Glendale, Arizona; Mike Ricksgers of Saxonburg, Pennsylvania; Tom Pietras of Battle Creek, Michigan; Ted M. O'Neal of Wilmington, North Carolina; Gina Guerrieri of Shawnee, Oklahoma; Jean Harrington of New York, New York; Oree C. Weller of Bellevue, Washington; and many others.

Why Are Weigh Stations on Highways Always Closed? Why Bother Building So Many of Them?

Drivers of overweight trucks have two big advantages over the enforcement officers at weigh stations: mobility and technology.

If every weigh station were open all the time, law-abiding truckers would be slowed intolerably. If the stations were spaced further apart but were always manned, canny drivers would take a circuitous route to bypass the weigh station. Because the weigh station is by definition stationary, and truckers almost always have an optional route to bypass the stations, state highway officials must find tactics to counter the mobility of the overweight trucks.

The technology that gives an advantage to the truckers is the citizens' band radio. Perhaps the CB is no longer a national fad, but it is still the primary source of intelligence for truckers. With truckers informing those behind them of where open weigh stations are located, keeping one weigh station open for a long period of time makes as much sense as printing the location of the weigh stations at the state border.

So how do officials strike back? By reclaiming the element of surprise. David J. Hensing, deputy executive director of the American Association of State Highway and Transportation Officials, told *Imponderables* that weigh stations are typically operated in the range of "an average of four hours a week at random times, although the level of use can vary widely from state to state and from station to station." By constantly shifting enforcement personnel, truckers are less likely to have fresh information about the location of open weigh stations, and by randomizing the staffing patterns, states make it impossible for truckers to figure out when weigh stations are open. The officials have found it more cost-effective to build 20 weigh stations open only 5 percent of the time than to build one station open all the time, and this method catches many more overweight trucks.

Officials are fighting back in other ways too. Many states are increasing their use of temporary scales that are set up at random times and locations and are experimenting with weigh-in-motion technologies that can weigh a truck without the driver knowing it.

So the next time you pass the "WEIGH STATION" sign with the "CLOSED" strip below it, rest assured that your enforcement officials are not off fishing, but somewhere else down the road doing their job.

Submitted by William Lush of Stamford, Connecticut.

Frustables

The 10 Most Wanted OR Imponderables

"Frustables" is short for "frustrating Imponderables," mysteries that have defied our frequent efforts to answer them. It isn't easy for us to admit that we can't hit a home run every time. In fact, sometimes we can't even lay down a sacrifice bunt. Sure, we've found some fascinating theories or bits of evidence that might lead to an answer to the ten Frustables you are about to read. But we don't have the proof to publish any answers.

So we throw our fragile ego onto the collective expertise and brilliance of our readers. Can you help? As always, we offer a reward of a free, autographed copy of the next volume of *Imponderables,* as well as an acknowledgment for your help in alleviating our frustration, to the first person who can lead to the proof that solves any of these Frustables. If you seek inspiration, following this section you can see how readers contended with the Frustables posed in *When Do Fish Sleep?*

Good luck with these new Frustables. You'll need it.

FRUSTABLE 1: *Does Anyone Really Like Fruitcake?*

We get some variation of this question quite frequently: Why does fruitcake exist? Why do nonprofit organizations sell fruitcakes for fundraisers when no one likes fruitcake? Why do people give fruitcakes as presents? (And yes, we've heard the story that there is only one fruitcake in the world which gets passed from person to person).

There might not be one definitive answer to such a complex phenomenon. But can anyone explain the proliferation of a product that no one seems to want? Or are there readers out there brave enough to publicly profess their love of fruitcake? Maybe we could publish your address and have all the unopened fruitcakes of the world sent to you.

FRUSTABLE 2: *Why Does the Stroking of Index Fingers Against Each Other Mean "Tsk-Tsk"?*

Why the stroking motion? Why not, say, the ring fingers?

FRUSTABLE 3: *We Often Hear the Cliché: "We Only Use 10 Percent of Our Brains." How Was It Determined that We Use 10 Percent and Not 5 Percent or 15 Percent?*

Is there any scientific basis for this claim? If so, who made it and when was it established.

FRUSTABLE 4: *Where, Exactly, Did the Expression "Blue Plate Special" Come from?*

We assume that there was a restaurant that actually did serve specials on blue plates. But where the heck was it?

FRUSTABLE 5: *Why Does the Traffic in Big Cities in the United States Seem Quieter than in Big Cities in Other Parts of the World?*

The transportation officials we spoke to denied that the premise is true. But this question from a reader confirms our experiences, too. Any ideas?

FRUSTABLE 6: *Why Do Dogs Tilt Their Heads When You Talk to Them?*

When we were researching out title Imponderable, we asked many experts what they thought about this Frustable. Several mentioned that dogs do not tilt their heads when listening to each other "arf." Why do cocker spaniels cock their heads when listening to our cockeyed ravings?

FRUSTABLE 7: *Why and Where Did the Notion Develop that "Fat People Are Jolly?"*

From Santa Claus to Mama Cass, this stereotype is rampant. Why?

FRUSTABLE 8: *Why Do Pigs Have Curly Tails?*

We've been trying to find an answer to this since *Why Do Clocks Run Clockwise?* Does the curl serve any function whatsoever?

FRUSTABLE 9: *Why Does the Heart Depicted in Illustrations Look Totally Different than a Real Heart?*

Where did the fanciful shape come from?

FRUSTABLE 10: *Where Do All the Missing Pens Go?*

Not to be confused with the missing sock issue, the problem of misplaced pens seems far more serious to us. Everyone we talked to thinks that they are a "net" loser of socks. So who picks up all the pens that we all lose? What happens to them? Will the person or persons who has all our pens admit it? Or give them back?

Frustables Update

As this book is being written, eight months have passed since the publication of *When Do Fish Sleep?* in hardbound, so readers of the paperback edition haven't had a chance yet to solve the ten Frustables posed in it. We've been flooded with responses to some of the Frustables but a few Frustables have attracted only a trickle.

So this section will often be a progress report rather than the last word on many of these Frustables. In the next volume of *Imponderables*, we promise to keep you informed of any breakthroughs in our neverending endeavor to stamp out Frustability. We also encourage any readers of this book who haven't read *When Do Fish Sleep?* to add your comments to these 10 Frustables.

Our thanks to all who contributed their solutions, especially those we haven't been able to include by name.

FRUSTABLE 1: *Why is Legal Paper 8½″ × 14″?*

What is especially frustrating about this Frustable is that the question seems like it would yield an easy answer. Yet the legal historians and paper companies we've contacted haven't been able to answer it. Even answers like Amboy, Washington, Kenneth McGoffin's—"Because it makes perfectly balanced paper airplanes"—started to sound good to us.

We heard from Dana Walker, of Ampad, a division of Mead Company, who claims that Ampad was the first company to produce the legal pad, at the beginning of the twentieth century:

> A Durham judge, tiring of penciling horizontal lines on scratch pads, wanted printed lines and a left vertical line for his marginal notes. So a hurried trip to the founder of the American Pad &

Paper Co., at Holyoke, produced the #369 legal pad of today, #369 because [Ampad's] Mr. Bockmiller lost first $3, then $6, then won $9 the previous night at poker.

Peter Bishop, Ampad's manager of marketing, confirms that the #369 pad measured 8″ × 14″, but can't explain the rationale behind the extra three-inch length.

Many readers speculated that the extra length was there to provide room for legal signatures (more cynical types insisted the extra length was there to compensate for lawyers' uncalled-for verbosity). But the most convincing argument came from one of our favorite correspondents, Fred Beeman, who lives in beautiful Kahului, Hawaii:

> When legal briefs were originally prepared in the early days of the U.S. legal system (on standard 8½″ × 11″ paper), there was never enough room at the bottom of the page for the notary public to place his statement of certification, and to emboss his seal, thus giving authenticity to a particular document. This could not be done on a separate piece of paper; it had to be done on the actual document itself.
>
> The more enterprising notaries would simply make their certifications on a separate sheet of paper (near the topmost portion). With scissors, they would cut off the top portion and use adhesive tape to affix that certification to the original document. Others, not as enterprising, would simply return the entire document(s) to the client, saying, "Leave approx. 3″ at the bottom for my certifications!".
>
> Eventually, some bright individuals decided that the solution was simply to make court documents about 3″ longer, so the "certification space" would already be there, and instruct secretaries to prepare documents as if the paper were 8½″ × 11″ in length.
>
> This worked. Secretaries would prepare documents as before, and the 3″ space would be at the bottom when the document was removed from the typewriter for a judge's signature, notarization, or whatever.

We can't verify this theory, but it's certainly the most plausible we've heard.

Maybe our favorite piece of correspondence concerning this Frustable came from the Association of Records Managers and Administrators' Project ELF ("Eliminate Legal-Size Files"). The lobbying efforts of Project ELF helped convince the Judicial Conference of the U.S. to adopt letter-size paper ($8\frac{1}{2}'' \times 11''$) as a standard in all Federal Courts, effective January 1, 1983. Most state court systems have followed suit. Project ELF claims that the costs of duplicating paper sizes and then housing correspondence in needlessly large file cabinets can increase the administrative operating cost of business and government up to 25 percent.

Submitted by Tristan MacAvery of Davis, California. Thanks also to William B. Katz of Highland Park, Illinois; Lisa Lipson of Sacramento, California; Joseph S. Blake, Jr. of Ottawa, Kansas; Joey Garman of Hanover, Pennsylvania; Jerry Kiewe of Lauderdale Lakes, Florida; Major Harry Malone of Lawton, Oklahoma; and Richard B. Stacy of Tucson, Arizona.

A free book goes to Fred T. Beeman of Kahului, Hawaii.

FRUSTABLE 2: *Why Do Americans, Unlike Europeans, Switch Forks to the Right Hand After Cutting Meat?*

We received several impassioned letters, defending the American style of switching hands. We still don't think it makes any sense, even if *we* switch hands, too.

Most of the serious theories boiled down to three camps. The first group saw the fork switching as an attempt to do what most table etiquette attempts—separating humans from their natural tendency to gorge as much food as quickly as possible. Perhaps Pat Steigman of Tyler, Texas, put it best:

> By having to switch hands, the diner is forced to put down his knife before eating the bite. Since he is not allowed to cut more than one bite at a time, he will again be forced to switch hands after the bite is eaten to cut his next bite. All of this hand switching is meant to slow down the eating process to a socially acceptable speed. Now, with just a glance, it is easy to discern those of proper breeding at the dinner table.

The most popular answer to this Frustable dates the custom back to the American Revolution and an interesting conspiracy theory. Judy Swierczak of Lahaina, Hawaii, offers her version:

> ... it developed as a secret signal during the American Revolution. It allowed other Revolutionaries to recognize their compatriots when dining in a group. If you all switched cutlery, then it was safe to talk about your activities. If some didn't switch, everyone kept their mouths shut. It was an innocuous gesture, but highly significant.

Although about ten readers offered this theory, none were able to cite sources for this information. Sounds apocryphal to us.

We buy a third theory, which is that until the mid-1700s, America was a forkless society. Hand switching, then, was once not a matter of manners but of necessity. Several readers told us about references to this subject in archaeologist James Deetz's *In Small Things Forgotten,* James Cross Giblin's *From Hand to Mouth,* and J. C. Furnas' *The Americans: A Social History of the United States 1587–1914.* We also found a short discussion of the subject in David E. Sutherland's *The Expansion of Everyday Life.*

Lou-Ann Rogers of Bethlehem, Pennsylvania, summarizes Giblin's explanation:

> ...forks did not come to America until the mid-1700s. Until that time, people used spoons and knives. Initially the knives were sharp and were used to stab meat—the spoon pressed the meat down while it was being cut and lifted to the mouth (yes, on the knife!).
>
> Then the sharp knives were replaced by rounded knives [we explained how this happened in Europe in *Imponderables*] that couldn't be used to transfer cut meat to the mouth. Thus, the spoon was still used to hold onto the meat while cutting it but then the knife was laid aside, the spoon put into the right hand and used to take the meat to the mouth. When forks came to the New World, people kept switching the way they had when using spoons.

Dale Neiburg of Laurel, Maryland, adds that forks, (which, like all cutlery, were imported from Europe) were not plentiful in the United States until the mid-1800s, whereas Europeans quickly integrated forks as an eating utensil:

Europeans, who went straight from knife to fork, hold the fork—and unconsciously think of it—as a modified knife. Americans, who went through an intervening "spoon phase," think of the fork and use it as a modified spoon.

Neiburg's theory also explains why Europeans generally hold their fork tines down, while Americans point the tines upward.

Although we may never find direct, conclusive proof of the "missing fork" theory, it sure beats anything else we've heard.

Submitted by Shirley Keller of Great Neck, New York. Thanks also to Peter DeMuth of Denver, Colorado; Robert W. Purdin of Tinton Falls, New Jersey; Ronald Walker of Covina, California; and Abner Fein of Wantagh, New York.

A free book goes to Lou-Ann Rogers of Bethlehem, Pennsylvania.

FRUSTABLE 3: *How, When, and Why Did the Banana Peel Become the Universal Slipping Agent in Vaudeville and Movies?*

Progress Report: No progress at all. Help!

FRUSTABLE 4: *Why did the Grade E Disappear from Grading Scales in Most Schools?*

We heard from a lot of you about this one, and it became abundantly clear that grading scales vary throughout the United States and have been changing at least since the turn of the century.

Only one theory was advanced that could explain why just about all school systems have eradicated the E from report cards. And we must admit that we were too innocent and ethical to have ever thought of the suggestion of Patti A. Willis of Endicott, New York, and many other readers:

Back in the old days, when report cards were hand-written and not a computer printout, a simple stroke of the pen could turn a

　　　　WHY DO DOGS HAVE WET NOSES?

failing grade, F, into an excellent grade, E. The temptation was just too great for some children to resist.

In Endicott, E equals excellence. But in many school districts, E meant one slim step above failure. Russell Tremayne, a retired high school teacher from Auburn, Washington, told how and why the E was banished from his system:

> A, B, C, D, and F were performance grades, indicating how a student had worked. They could be used as grades of record, entered upon a school transcript. The E, however, was a predictive comment, a sort of early warning. While the E could be used on the report card at midterm, it could not be used as a semester grade; it had to be converted to an F on the final transcript.
>
> Trying to evaluate at midterm, a teacher was in a quandary as to how to grade a borderline student. If he gave the pupil an E, "a warning of possible failure," the student's response was usually the negative, "If I'm failing, I'll quit working."
>
> If the teacher, trying to encourage the student, gave him a D and then, seeing the student slack off severely, gave him an F at semester time, the student (and often his parents) would cry foul, claiming that the teacher could not give a final F without having issued an interim E warning.
>
> So the troublesome E was banished, and administrators, teachers, parents, and pupils were retaught that a D meant passing but in danger of failing should work deteriorate. A student could go from a D at midterm to an F at the semester's end without statistical contradiction or anyone's emotional flip-out.

Jeff Gay of Middleboro, Massachusetts, and Kenneth N. Burgess of Oakdale, Louisiana, report that at one time in their school systems, E also indicated a failing performance but one that showed effort.

But the majority of the correspondents felt that the E was eliminated to avoid confusion between E as a low grade and E as "excellent." Pamela L. Gibson of Belleville, New Jersey, mentioned that her elementary school used an E(xcellent), V(ery) G(ood), S(atisfactory), P(oor), and U(nsatisafactory) system. Gibson believes that "the A through F system was abolished in my school to prevent children from being traumatized by receiving the dreaded F."

Charles Northrop sent us his 1965–1966 report card from Campbell, California, with an unusual system of E (outstanding work), S+ (very satisfactory progress), S (progress compares favorably with ability), S− (below expected progress), and N (needs improvement, capable of doing much better). But J. Orrville Smith beats Charles by almost fifty years with our first reported use of E as excellent. He attended elementary school in Portsmouth, Virginia, from 1918 to 1926, where the grading scale was E(xcellent), V(ery) G(ood), G(ood), F(air), P(oor), and, ignominiously, V(ery) P(oor).

We heard from Tom Schoeck, who has spent more than 35 years working in education. He attended a private elementary school with an interesting grading policy:

> Academic subjects were graded, in descending order, A–B–C–D–F, while the non-academic areas (gym, music, art, and most important—"comportment"—later called "conduct") were graded E–S–U, for Excellent, Satisfactory and Unsatisfactory.
>
> Heaven forfend we should ever bring home a report card with a U in conduct! My understanding is that the E–S–U system predated the A–F system and was earlier in use for all subjects. But with the need or opportunity for more objectively precise sorting of students' performance levels arising sometime between the turn of the century and World War I (or even earlier in some areas of the country), somewhat "finer" classifications were needed. All this has been solved now, of course, with the emergence of numerical equivalents for letter grades, the 4.0 system, bell curves, standard deviations, etc.

Perhaps our favorite letter on this Frustable comes from Mike Schramm of Syracuse, New York, who demonstrates that an ingenious, underachieving student can make the best out of a failing grade, providing his parents are sufficiently credulous:

> My father went to high school in Rochester, New York, in the late 1930s and early 1940s. His report cards showed a grading system with A, B, C, D, and E (with no F's).

When I asked him about E, he said that some kids were able to convince their parents that E meant "excellent." This made for embarrassing confrontations with parents who thought their children were doing just fine, only to be told otherwise. A parent who would believe this might be likely to have a child who would get a lot of E's.

A free book goes to Mike Schramm of Syracuse, New York, for making us laugh.

FRUSTABLE 5: *How Did They Lock Saloon Doors in the Old West?*

Most of the many people who wrote us about this Frustable gained their knowledge about saloon doors not from historical research but from westerns on TV and movies or from visits to theme parks. Just about everyone knew that the swinging doors were not all that separated the saloon from Front Street, but only David Di Mattia of Yonkers, New York, worried about whether all of his totally logical explanations were less important than the needs of the entertainment industry:

> The swinging door was not the only door that shared the same door frame. When saloons were closed, full-length double doors (with or without pane glass) were used to provide security after business hours or on days closure was mandated by blue laws.
>
> The swinging saloon door served a few purposes for such a business establishment. Its half-length allowed patrons to see incoming or existing customers while still providing a modest amount of privacy for those imbibing inside. They also allowed for continuous air flow to help alleviate smoke and heat build-up during peak business hours. Finally, *maybe the swinging doors provided a safe throughway for movie and TV stuntmen.*

The only problem with the solutions proposed by almost everyone who wrote is that they were wrong. Our old friend, historian and writer C. F. "Charley" Eckhardt, who specializes in the American West, wrote:

The swinging doors of a Western saloon are the exterior doors only in Hollywood. If you'll take a magnifying glass to "Front Street" pictures of almost any western town, you'll find that most saloons had ordinary front doors like every other business in town.

Yes, saloons *did* have swinging doors—but they didn't open onto the street. *In most saloons, you entered through an ordinary lockable door at the front.* This brought you into the "cigar apartment," where the owner-manager's private offices were usually located and where you could buy cigars and package liquors—bottles wrapped in brown paper and tied with a string. There was then a partition, sometimes very elaborate, often scrollworked and leaded-glassed, with a pair of swinging doors in it. When you went through the swinging doors, you went from the cigar apartment into the saloon proper.

Eckhardt sent us photocopies of the *Brunswick–Balke–Collender Illustrated Catalog of Bar Fixtures, 1891,* including a floor plan for a single-story, single-lot saloon, that clearly shows that the swinging doors separate the saloon from the cigar apartment, not the street; the swinging doors cannot be seen from the outside. So much for the ventilation and privacy theories.

If you want to see examples of saloon exteriors, Charles Gerald Melton of Providence, Rhode Island, sent us a letter indicating that there are several verbal and pictorial references to saloons in the Time-Life *Old West* series. Pictures in *The Loggers, The Rivermen,* and *The Townsmen* show saloons with nonswinging exterior doors, although Melton points out that many kept their doors open 24 hours a day.

Ann Calhoun of Los Osos, California, won't be dissuaded by something so flimsy as hard evidence, though. She provided a fanciful history of the swinging door in saloons. She claims that the swinging doors were substitutes for curtains that were originally placed on the bottom half of saloons' windows to block the view inside. And somehow, she has managed to make this a feminist, ageist, and temperance issue:

> If you've ever noticed, swinging doors are always placed a few inches below the eye level of the average adult male, which

would put them a few inches above the eye level of the average adult female and completely block the view of the average whippersnapper. Unless, of course, he faked a broken shoelace at the precise moment of passing the forbidden door, bent down and *then* caught a glimpse of the nekkid lady over the bar.

As civilization progressed (?), electricity powered overhead fans, glass windows became cheap and plentiful, God invented air conditioning and swinging doors soon disappeared (unless the establishment was going all Yuppie, trendy, and thematic-kitschy), only to be replaced by often incredibly ornate sand-blasted glass windows and doors. Yet the theory still remained: If you're tall enough to see above the swinging doors, you're old enough to go inside and buy yourself a drink. If not, go home and have a nice glass of milk and some of Mommy's cookies.

Even today, ever walk past a self-respecting saloon, one worthy of the name? The place resembles a bunker expecting incoming artillery rounds! The only time the front door is *ever* open is when they're closed for business, the help is mopping the floors and swilling out the toilets and they desperately need cross ventilation lest the workers become stricken by the Lysol fumes . . .

So you can't trust everything you see on television or movies! How did they lock saloons in the Old West? With keys.

Submitted by Maria Katinos of Los Angeles, California.

A free book goes to C. F. Eckhardt of Seguin, Texas.

FRUSTABLE 6: *Why Do So Many People Save* National Geographics *and Then Never Look at Them Again?*

"What is this Frustable?" moaned reader Ann Calhoun, who waxed freely over Frustable 5. "Do I look like a psychiatrist?"

Well, no. In fact, this Frustable, which drew more mail than all but number 10, attracted dozens of different explanations for why people save the magazine, but few readers would play armchair shrink and speculate about why we save reading material that we will never pick up again.

We even got a few letters from folks who claimed that they actually did go back and read old *NG*s. Sure. But most Frustable-busters spoke with the detachment of cultural anthropologists.

The most popular response was that in almost every way, *National Geographics* resemble books to be saved indefinitely rather than disposable magazines. As evidence, they point to:

- the flat spine
- the volume numbers and subjects, printed on the spine for easy reference, implying the issues are meant to be saved
- the glued binding

- the heavy, glossy paper stock
- foldout maps
- their ability to stand up like books
- and of course, the exquisite coffee-table booklike color photography

We also heard from students and parents of students, perhaps most entertainingly from four Oregon State University students: Tara Boehler, Brenda Miller, Krista Hess, and Jennifer Crocker:

> We are always encountering maniacal instructors who assign outrageously long and detailed papers (due by the end of the week) that require not only research but also visual aids. So we trot to our closets or under our beds and drag out the ole *National Geographic* stack and start cutting.

In support of the OSU contingent, William Kelso adds that the subject matter of *National Geographic* makes them worth having around: "An article on a geographic area or species of animal will still be more or less valid ten years later."

Mike Babin, technical services librarian of the Port Arthur [Texas] Library, reports that people actually do read back issues of *NG*:

> ... they just don't read *their* copies. *National Geographic* is not self-indexed ... it's much easier and convenient to go to your local library, which does have the index, and find the article wanted. I've found that most people are very good about remembering that they've read an article in the magazine, but not so good about remembering when they read it.

So much for the invaluable subject headings and volume and number notations on the flat spine of the magazine that were the excuse for saving the issues in the first place.

So if most of the people who subscribe to and save *National Geographics* don't reread them, why do they save them? Ann Calhoun, our reluctant psychiatrist, turns unrepentant capitalist and suggests that the thinking runs along the lines of "Better hold onto these—someday they're going to be worth a lot of money." Little do these hoarders know that hundreds of thousands of others are simultaneously trying to dump their collections upon a yawning public.

H. E. Todd of Portland, Oregon, and others suggest that perhaps saving *NG*s has something in common with keeping old *Playboy* and *Penthouse* collections, although Todd admits that the latter have "higher frontal nudity density."

Paul Ruggerio of Blacksburg, Virginia, was not the only but certainly the youngest reader (at age 12) to suggest that shelves full of *National Geographic* have a certain snob appeal. Paul tells us not to feel inferior when we see a shelf full of the magazine in a neighbor's house:

> Don't let it get to you because deep down, you know that your secret stash of yellow magazines is sending the same message. And besides, they've never read any of their *National Geographics* either.

Perhaps we are cockeyed idealists, but we would like to think that the untold stacks of *National Geographics* are testimony to the noblest yearnings of the human spirit (and to the most Western of all negative emotions—guilt). We go along with reader William Kelso:

> The subject material of *National Geographic* is informative, educational, and uplifting: the sort of thing *we know we should be reading*. But other things always seem more pressing—quarterly sales results, centerfolds in skin magazines, etc. So we tell ourselves that we'll keep the *Geographics* and read them when we get around to it. Guilt is what keeps them on the shelf.

The same process (along with a healthy dose of laziness) also explains why 90 percent of our books remain on our shelves at home. How many of the books in your collection have you reread? What makes you think you will go back to the novel that you couldn't make it halfway through in high school—especially when you know you won't be tested on it?

Submitted by Wendy Rath of Sandy, Utah.

A free book goes to William Kelso of Mercer Island, Washington.

FRUSTABLE 7: Why Do People, Especially Kids, Tend to Stick Their Tongues Out When Concentrating?

Those of you who based your responses on pure speculation were clearly floundering. You probably didn't realize that actual scientific research has been conducted on this subject. Two strong theories emerge that have little in common with each other:

1. Sticking out the tongue is an unconscious signal to onlookers to stay away. Deborah Ledwich of Arthur, Ontario, was the first to write us about this:

> Whenever we see a person concentrating on something with the tip of his tongue protruding, we tend to be reluctant to speak to him or disturb him. Therefore, the sticking out of the tongue is a psychological signal (from the person who is concentrating on his task) to other people that he is busy and doesn't want to be disturbed. It works very effectively most of the time, too.

Experiments conducted with teachers indicated that students were less likely to approach the desk of the teacher when the teacher had his or her tongue sticking out.

Chances are, the students didn't consciously register the tongue position of their teacher, but the process may be unconscious for the "tonguer" and the "tonguee." We find one major problem with this theory, though—it doesn't explain why people still stick out their tongues when they are alone.

2. Remember Lily Tomlin's Edith-Ann character, the little girl who stuck her tongue out when concentrating? We heard from several people who indicated that there was a physiological explanation for the wayward tongue. Evan A. Ballard and E. Wilson Griffin III, two physicians at the Jonesville Family Medical Center in Jonesville, North Carolina, were the first and most qualified to discuss this theory. Here's what they wrote:

> Why do Michael Jordan and other talented human beings (including my five-year-old son) wiggle and waggle a pro-

truding tongue while performing tasks requiring concentration and dexterity?

The answer lies in the location in the brain of control of hands and mouths. The cerebral cortex is the site in the brain where complicated tasks and thoughts are integrated. Each part of the body is represented in the cerebral cortex at a certain area. It so happens that the area of the cortex controlling the tongue is immediately adjacent to the area controlling the hands. [Does this reasoning sound familiar? It's virtually the same explanation for the Frustable we answered in *When Do Fish Sleep?:* Why does looking up at the sun cause many people to sneeze?]

The reason for this is more than simply coincidence. Theory has it that man evolved his incredible dexterity with his hands (especially his opposable thumb) as he was developing his speech capacity. Speech, of course, requires much dexterity of the tongue and mouth in general. Since the areas of the brain controlling the hand and the mouth are adjacent to each other as well as performing closely related functions, many of their neurological pathways are interconnected. Activity in the neurons controlling the hand often leads, inadvertently, to activity in neurons controlling the mouth.

The tongue and the hands, therefore, are extremely closely related functionally and spatially in the brain, even though they are at some distance from each other in the body. Does this explain why some of us find our hands producing wild gestures when we are earnestly trying to express ourselves verbally?

Adding fuel to Ballard and Griffin's theory is the observation that many musicians stick out their tongue when doing fine picking (e.g., Roy Clark, B. B. King).

Why do kids, in particular, tend to stick out their tongues? Probably because they haven't yet learned that it is socially unacceptable behavior.

Finally, we can't resist sharing a story sent to us by H. E. Todd:

My daughter, a physician, was sticking out her tongue while water skiing one day. Asked if she did this when performing a difficult medical procedure and if so, if it might interfere with patient confidence, she replied, "Why do you think we doctors wear masks?"

Submitted by Malinda Fillingion of Savannah, Georgia. Thanks also to Ruby Clasby of Federal Way, Washington.

A free book goes to Drs. Evan A. Ballard and E. Wilson Griffin III of Jonesville, North Carolina; and Deborah Ledwich of Arthur, Ontario.

FRUSTABLE 8: *Why Do Kids Tend to Like Meat Well Done (and Then Prefer It Rarer and Rarer as They Get Older)?*

Two main schools of thought predominated, with many supporters for each. But there was precious little evidence to support either of these theories:

1. Kids associate rare meat with blood and, unconsciously, the fact that they are eating a once-living animal. But how does this explain why kids lose this fear as they get older?
2. Kids have extremely sensitive taste buds and prefer the blander taste of a burnt burger to the gamy taste of a rare piece of meat. Maybe. But the taste experts we consulted couldn't find any evidence to support this theory.

Anybody have a better explanation, or hard evidence, to support either of these two theories?

FRUSTABLE 9: *Why Does Whistling at an American Sporting Event Mean "Yay!" When Whistling Means "Boo!" in Most Other Countries?*

Never has a Frustable bored so many. The few speculations we received are too lame to report to a family audience. Do we have any anthropologists out there who can help us with this one? We can't seem to get to first base (boo!) on this one.

FRUSTABLE 10: *Why Are So Many Restaurants, Especially Diners and Coffee Shops, Obsessed with Mating Ketchup Bottles at the End of the Day?*

In *When Do Fish Sleep?*, we whined about our problem hailing a waitress to take our order because she was too busy stacking ketchup bottles. We questioned whether customers really care about having full bottles of ketchup in front of them. After all, half-full bottles flow more easily. Why do restaurateurs demand that their staff waste their time with this time-consuming activity?

We were deluged with responses. We heard from restaurateurs, waiters, and waitresses, but especially from *ex*-waiters and *ex*-waitresses, a contingent large enough to form a politically powerful lobbying group if they ever got organized.

They let us know in no uncertain terms that mating ketchup bottles was far from their favorite activity. But they were pressured to, as it is variously called, "mate," "marry," "stack," or "consolidate" ketchup bottles at the end of their shifts. The letter from Barrie Creedon of Philadelphia, Pennsylvania, was typical:

In any restaurant, "side work," any work you are not paid for (e.g., cleaning, stocking, stacking) is a major source of hostility among the staff. The opening crew thinks the closing crew is a bunch of lazy slobs and vice versa.

However, it is my experience that the biggest, toughest, most terrifying waitresses are always on the opening shift [remember, the thoughts expressed in this letter do not necessarily reflect the sentiments of the author, who has the utmost respect and veneration for opening-shift waitresses]. And if their ketchup bottles aren't nice and clean when they take them from the refrigerator, they can become *extremely* unhappy. So you work like there's no tomorrow on the bottles the night before in case there is a tomorrow, because if one of these women gets mad, it's not a pretty sight.

Many correspondents insisted that customers do indeed prefer full bottles, perhaps because the customer perceives a clean, full bottle as new. Annie Lloyd of Mercer, California, argues the case:

> No one wants to use anything, including ketchup, that hundreds of strangers have used before him. So keeping the ketchup bottles full give the customer the illusion of having a new bottle that no one else has used prior to his arrival.

Kate Levander of Minneapolis, Minnesota, explains why it's so hard to catch the attention of a waiter when a coffee shop is about to close:

> Ketchup bottles, unlike humans, take a long time before the mating process is complete. It takes quite a while for the inverted top bottle to glop all the ketchup into the bottom bottle.
>
> Waiters and waitresses just don't want to wait until the lower ketchup bottles are full so they can go home. They have been *waiting* all day—on people asking for more ketchup.

Levander adds that while it may be true that full bottles of ketchup are slower to pour for the customer, half-full bottles make the marrying process much faster for the waiters.

Many restaurants do not simply consolidate the contents of

used bottles and replace them with factory-sealed bottles. Heinz and many other brands sell large #10 cans and two-gallon bags of ketchup for restaurant use; however, these large containers are not designed for use in refilling used bottles. Beth Adams, of Heinz public communications, says that her company does not condone the practice for hygienic reasons.

But this doesn't stop most restaurants. Heidi Cheney of Caldwell, Idaho, wrote us that the restaurant in which she worked used a funnel to collect upended bottles and poured the collected ketchup into [we hope] rinsed, recycled bottles.

All but the tackiest eateries do try to rinse off bottles. But Beth Adams observed that she has seen bottle necks cleaned with dirty rags. Not too hygienic.

Let's face it. The bottom line on this Frustable is the bottom line. Restaurants can save money by consolidating. Henry Verden, a professional restaurant manager from Elmhurst, Illinois, explains:

> #10 cans are much cheaper than buying smaller 10- or 12-ounce bottles. Since large cans would be, to say the least, impractical on tables, the restaurant will make an initial investment in bottles and then refill them from the #10 cans. Refilling ketchup bottles then becomes simply a matter of restocking every evening, just as you refill sugar shakers, napkin dispensers, and salt and pepper shakers.
>
> Stock rotation is the reason for "mating" the bottles. Simply refilling partial bottles would leave older ketchup in the bottom of every bottle. By combining partial bottles you leave empties to infuse fresh ketchup into the system without mixing it with old ketchup, which would shorten the shelf life of the fresher product. The bottles containing the older ketchup will be used up in the normal course of business.

Verden ends on an ominous note: "It also provides a manager with a project to keep waitresses, waiters, and bus people busy during slow periods."

And our saloon-door expert, Charley Eckhardt, who once owned a café, adds his two bits. If you don't use the big cans to dispense the ketchup, consolidating helps keep track of inventory: "Once you've consolidated the ketchup into as few bottles as possible, the empties tell you how much ketchup you've used and how much you need to buy." According to Beth Adams, one of the reasons Heinz is upset about ketchup "marriage" is that some less than reputable restaurants use Heinz bottles on the tables but fill them with off-brands in the kitchen. In this case, Heinz loses out twice: the restaurant buys neither the high-profit-margin 14-ounce bottles nor the bulk ketchup.

All this commotion, remember, is about ketchup, not exactly the most important element of any dining establishment. Melanie Morton of Branford, Connecticut, wrote us a particularly witty letter about her travails with ketchup mating. She writes that while demanding patrons are trying to flag a waitress at the end of her shift,

> she's tired, her feet hurt, and she wants to count her tips. And those precariously balanced bottles have a tendency to tip over when left unattended.
>
> . . . It's the wonderful details like this in the restaurant business that made me leave it.

A free book goes to Henry A. Verden of Elmhurst, Illinois, and Melanie Morton of Branford, Connecticut. And special thanks to the many other former and current waiters and waitresses who sent equally good letters.

LETTERS

We are used to receiving letters with criticisms or corrections, but not from folks saying that our title was wrong!

In the early 1800s, the Waterbury Clock Co. of Waterbury, Connecticut, offered for sale a clock much like the Seth Thomas school clock. The main difference is that the Waterbury clock ran counterclockwise. The dial was made with the numerals fixed backwards.

These clocks were hung on the rear wall of barber shops. With the customer sitting in the barber chair facing large mirrors, the clock appeared "normal."

The Waterbury Clock Co. was destroyed by fire in 1880.

JOHN PARISEAU
Jewett City, Connecticut

But the concept lives on:

To be absolutely correct, the title of your book should be *Why Do MOST Clocks Run Clockwise?* . . . A barbershop clock which runs counterclockwise is still sold by a company named Klockit, in Lake Geneva, Wisconsin . . .

PAUL J. KRAHE
Erie, Pennsylvania

In When Do Fish Sleep?, *we answered an Imponderable about why automobiles require separate keys for the ignition and doors. We heard from a reader who thought two keys might be two keys too few:*

My old 1958 Chevy Yeoman station wagon had no less than *four* keys: ignition; doors; glovebox; and tailgate. The keys were all square-headed, too—you couldn't tell them apart by touch in the dark, like you can with modern keys.

The keys came in handy once, though. Some smart aleck in a '61 Impala parked behind me, blocking me in a parking space. My tailgate key fit his doors and my glovebox key fit his ignition. I drove his car about half a block, parked it by a fireplug and locked it up.

CHARLEY ECKHARDT
Seguin, Texas

In When Do Fish Sleep?, *we wrote about an accountant named Walter Diemer who invented bubble gum. But we erred in calling him an entrepreneur. A relative of Mr. Diemer's wrote to clarify:*

Mr. Diemer, who is 85 and lives in Lancaster, was a cost accountant with the Fleer Corporation. The company was attempting to develop its own base for making gum, and the lab was right near his office. He discovered that some of the rubber base mixes bubbled when chewed and set about systematically varying ingredients until he came up with one that chewed well and bubbled consistently. He had no knowledge of either chemistry or food. His finding was serendipitous and the development of the finished product the result of a great deal of trial and error experimentation.

BRUCE C. WITTMAIER
Lancaster, Pennsylvania

In When Do Fish Sleep?, *we discussed why only older men seem to have hairy ears. We allowed a misstatement by a reader to pass without notice. Several readers wrote us with thoughts similar to the following letter:*

I must dispute the comment that color blindness and pattern baldness are traits of the Y chromosome. Actually, the opposite is true. The most common forms of color blindness (those affecting the green and red cones), the two most common forms of hemophilia, and pattern baldness are all traits of the X chromosome. Then why are these problems generally associated with men? Because women, who have two X chromosomes, have two chances of getting a good allele, while men have only one.

DAVID S. RALEY
Germantown, Maryland

In Why Do Clocks Run Clockwise?, *we discussed why there "21 guns" in a 21-gun salute. Several readers were disturbed with the fact that we didn't make it clear that there are 21 SHOTS in the salute, not necessarily 21 separate guns. We couldn't resist sharing this story passed along by a reader about a supposed Commodore Joseph E. Fyfe, who commanded a cruiser squadron operating in the Mediterranean during the closing years of the nineteenth century:*

> Fyfe brought his ships into Gibraltar early one morning and delivered the salute required by current regulations. The gunner of the flagship goofed and a salute of twenty-*two* guns was sounded.
>
> When reproached by the Brits for this gaffe, the Commodore replied that he had ordered 21 guns for Queen Victoria and one gun for Mrs. Joseph E. Fyfe.

JOHN H. KAUFMAN
Coronado, California

Although several doctors and several medical textbooks we consulted confirmed that those half-moons (lunulae) on our fingernails are white because of trapped air, we are ready to bow to the many doctors who wrote to us to disagree:

> . . . The lunula is the outermost, and therefore only visible, portion of the nail matrix. The rest of the matrix lies hidden beneath the proximal nail fold (the fold of tissue that ends in the cuticle).
>
> The function of the lunula, and the rest of the matrix, is well known: The matrix is what produces the nail plate (the nail itself). This is why the lunula never moves. New nail is continually formed, and continually pushed forward, away from the matrix.

DIRK M. ELSTON, M.D.
Newport News, Virginia

But why are lunulae white?

> The lunulae of nails are not white because of trapped air. The lunulae are white because the matrices of the nails lie beneath them—a different tissue from the nail beds.
>
> The nail beds distal to the lunulae look pink because capillaries with blood in them immediately underlie the nail plate. The lunulae look white because the thin, modified epidermis of the

nail bed is three or four times thicker there, being the busy factory where nail plate is manufactured. The lunula is avascular [without blood vessels], so it looks white.

HARRY L. ARNOLD, JR., M.D.

Although we received our information about the naming of Oreo cookies from several sources at Nabisco, a few readers took us to task for our explanation. We made a one-letter mistake in our spelling that might be crucial:

> ... The Greek word for "mountain" is *not* "oreo," but "oro." It makes me doubt that the cookies we know today had ever been shaped like mountains, or else they would be called *Oro* cookies.
>
> I have a Greek friend who has always insisted that the cookies must have been named by a Greek man, because the word *oreo* is, in fact, a word in modern Greek. *Oreo* means "nice," or "pleasant," even "appetizing."
>
> Seeing this familiar word on a cookie box is what originally prompted my friend to buy Oreos when he first came to America ...

KATHERINE CALDWELL
Crosswicks, New Jersey

Reader Richard Sassaman of Bar Harbor, Maine, was kind enough to send us a review of a book we had already read: The Pencil: A History of Design and Circumstance, *written by Henry Petroski. Petroski attributes the omnipresence of yellow pencils to the mid-nineteenth century, when pencil makers faced a shortage of graphite. A German company, A. W. Faber, found a new and exclusive source of superb graphite in Siberia, near the Chinese border. Faber's competitors, without access to Faber's stash, colored their pencils yellow to hint at the oriental association that only Faber actually enjoyed.*

In When Do Fish Sleep?, *we discussed why telephone cords seem to twist up spontaneously. One reader has a simple theory that makes sense to us:*

> Right-handed people answer the phone by picking it up with their right hand [not us, but we won't protest too vigorously].

WHY DO DOGS HAVE WET NOSES?

Typically, about thirty seconds to a minute into the conversation, though, they transfer the phone to their left ear in order to free their right hand to do other things, such as taking notes. When they put the phone down, presto! Exactly one twist has been added to the phone cord. This adds up rather quickly.

GEOFFREY A. LANDIS
Brook Park, Ohio

In our discussion of why the sound of running water in pipes changes as it gets hot (in Why Do Clocks Run Clockwise?*), we quoted a plumbing official who said that one of the reasons the phenomenon exists is "because of additional air in the hot water formed when the molecules expand during the heating process." Our source had it wrong. One of the many letters to correct this point came from a chemist at Purdue University:*

Nothing could be further from the truth. Molecules do not expand like Ballpark Franks. The explanation of the additional air in the hot water has its origin in the solubility of air itself in water. The solubility of air in water varies with the temperature of the water and the pressure of the gas above the water.

Therefore, as the temperature of the water increases, the solubility of the air in the water becomes lower. This would cause the air to come out of solution as a gas, hence the additional air in the hot water.

MARCY HAMBY
West Lafayette, Indiana

We discussed why women wear such uncomfortable shoes, especially high heels, in Imponderables. *We stressed highfalutin Freudian interpretations, but many women saw it as more of a feminist issue. We received a dissertation on the subject, part of which is found below:*

In heels, a woman stands with her weight centered on the balls of her feet. This throws forward the postural axis that normally runs down through the (anatomical) heels. In order to still stand straight, she must unconsciously make several muscular changes, which in concert tend to pull in her stomach, thrust out her behind, and tighten and emphasize her calves.

"What's wrong with that?" you ask malely. Not much, except

AND OTHER IMPONDERABLES 229

for the slight, continual, unnatural exertion required just to stand straight. The woman is not perfectly relaxed standing still, which has a subliminally inhibiting effect. She has few options for shifting her weight unobtrusively if she must stand for a long time (try it!), so she stands *still*. It's tiring, so she wants to sit down . . .

Now, walking in high heels. . . . The shoe heels hold up her feet's heel, but because her weight is pushed forward, she cannot rest it on her feet's heels as she walks. The effect is to shorten her stride and to bring her feet closer together with her toes nearly touching the imaginary line one might draw along between her footprints; to keep her balance she must exaggerate the transfer of weight from side to side. If she is still keeping her shoulders back and head up, she must swing her hips side to side; if she ignores her upper body, she's more likely either to lurch and fall forward or to buckle at the ankles and fall sideways . . .

LINDA DUPLANTIS
Bloomington, Indiana

So what does the "high-heel walk" mean? Linda Duplantis thinks the heels were meant to inhibit the movement of the women who wear them. If nothing else, most women prefer sitting down to hobbling on heels. A similar conclusion was echoed by another reader:

It is the preference of the heterosexual male for the high-heeled woman and her shapely legs and distinctive walk, and not necessarily a woman's vanity, that has caused the uncomfortable shoe to continue to flourish. Note the company policy within some corporations that all of its women executives are required to wear high heels. That isn't women's vanity; that's male ego and the desire to continue his sexual fantasies.

. . . Having a spinal disorder that requires that I wear flat shoes, it is interesting to note the cultural biases of men, women, the clothing industry, and employers to flat shoes. My personal observation, at 50+ years of age, is that there will never be sexual equality as long as women continue to wear high-heeled shoes. They probably will continue wearing them as long as men consider them attractive on a woman.

LINDA KIRKHAM WALTON
San Jose, California

WHY DO DOGS HAVE WET NOSES?

High heels weren't the only footwear you had on your mind. There are two Imponderables from Why Do Clocks Run Clockwise? *that just won't go away: Why do some ranchers hang old boots on fenceposts? And why do you so often find one shoe lying on the side of the road? Most of you who wrote about the boots repeated points made in our* When Do Fish Sleep? *Frustables Update, particularly the argument that the boots are there to prevent water rot. But we received several letters, mostly from Colorado and Wyoming, with another point:*

> I grew up on a ranch in the mountains of Colorado, and old boots were (and probably still are) hung on fenceposts. It was a tradition to hang the boots there when a new pair was purchased so that another ranchhand who might have been down on his luck, or for any reason had a worse pair of boots, could try them on. If they preferred your old boots, they could keep them or hang them back on the fence for someone else to try.
>
> Eventually someone would get sick of seeing the boots up there and take them down or tell one of the kids (usually me) to throw them away.
>
> MITCHELL DAVIS
> *Springfield, Virginia*

But not all our readers' stories about boots on fenceposts were quite so heartwarming:

> I once lived on a small farm with several friends. One day an unknown person placed a single old boot on our pasture fence. We took a liking to it and continued the practice, using the ubiquitous single shoes we would find along the road. Before too long, the entire length of pasture fence had a shoe on every post.
>
> It had been a few years since I moved, but upon returning for a visit I learned of some new developments. One night *all* the shoes mysteriously disappeared. A neighbor, noticing the absence, approached the house. Upon seeing my former roommates' dog—the recent recipient of a "punk" haircut—the neighbors decided it was all part of some kind of satanic ritual, and called the police.
>
> BILL COOK
> *Oakville, California*

AND OTHER IMPONDERABLES

Unfortunately, the police never seemed to catch the felons. The correspondence about the "one shoe" syndrome veers toward the bizarre. One reader spotted the article in the syndicated column "News of the Weird," about a business professor at a college in Dubuque, Iowa,

> . . . who stole shoes from students at universities in two states over a five-year period by snatching them in libraries when students left their tables for short breaks. . . .

The professor claimed he donated the pilfered shoes to the homeless, but police found 80 pairs of shoes in his apartment.

> . . . An apparently unrelated rash of shoe thefts (one shoe at a time) occurred in the Boston Public Library earlier last year.

> MRS. LOUISE RUSSELL
> Chicago, Illinois

And another reader can give a personal testimonial to the one-shoe theft epidemic that threatens the stability of the world as we know it:

> I used to work for Gold Circle, a discount store similar to K-Mart. I was a "price change associate." My job was to change price tags in all departments. Part of my job was daily restraightening of the various store sections and assistance in quarterly and annual inventories.
>
> During the two quarterly inventories and one annual inventory in which I participated, I found over 300 "pairs" (of various sizes and styles) missing the right or the left shoe. I questioned the department manager and store manager. They said, and had documented police reports to prove it, that many people in the past, rich and poor alike, had entered the store and taken only the right or left shoe. In some cases, they threw down their old worn out shoe and just walked out of the store.
>
> Since manufacturers will only sell pairs to a retail outlet and styles change so rapidly, the Gold Circle chain was stuck with an unusable stock item on the books. Each store was told to purge

WHY DO DOGS HAVE WET NOSES?

unusable stocks (i.e., throw in the trash) to make room for good stock and take a tax write-off . . .

JOSEPH A. RAUBAR
Amherst, New York

One daring gentleman tried to synthesize the two Imponderables that REFUSE TO DIE:

I can solve both Imponderables. The shoes lying by the side of roads fell off fenceposts! Or someone found a shoe on the side of the road and put it on a fencepost!

GREGORY REIS
Torrance, California

Our favorite letter of the last year proved to be a humbling one. It's bad enough to occasionally write a passage that other people can't understand. But what about when a reader asks a question about what we've written that proves that WE don't understand our own writing?:

I have read your book *When Do Fish Sleep?* to my children. On page 210 in the section on right- or left-hand driving, there is a puzzling sentence: "These pedestals [that once helped riders mount horses on public roadways] were found only on the left side of the road."

One of my sons asked which was the left side of a north-south road? The east or the west? The two boys hootingly averred that any fool knew it was east.

As a former air navigator, I was asked to arbitrate. I urged the children to think it over analytically and bring me the results. I then applied ointment, bandages, and one tourniquet to the results.

Please publish an answer soon. I'm running out of splints.

SAM E. STUBBS
Brampton, Ontario

Well, Mr. Stubbs, after reading your letter, we weren't feeling so well ourselves. But we felt much better after speaking to Richard Hopper, our main source for the answer to this Frustable. We did know one fact about the pedestals on roadways:

They were located adjacent to curbs but abutted houses (and buildings) and were used primarily by the occupants of those houses (and buildings).

According to Hopper, when a horse was led out to be mounted, the horse was already facing "left" so that it could be properly mounted from the left (nobody with any sense wants to mount a horse so that one's legs kick over the horse's head in the process). As we said in When Do Fish Sleep?, Hopper has found much evidence that both pedestrian and horse traffic had traditionally kept to the left anyway, so that the right hand could be used to wave a hand in friendly greeting or a knife in less friendly situations.

So the answer to Mr. Stubbs' children's question (Which was the left side of a north-south road?) is: It depends on which direction the horse is going. If the horse is heading north, then the left side is west; if the horse is heading south, the left side is east.

Mr. Stubbs, you may now remove your splints.

Acknowledgments

It's thank-you time again. And once again, my first and most important thanks go to you, the readers. Not just for buying the books but for sharing your Imponderables, your criticisms, your answers to the Frustables, and your words of encouragement. The only way I have of gauging what you like and don't like about the *Imponderables* books is by reading your letters. Your correspondence make my work worthwhile.

Harper & Row may have just transformed itself into HarperCollins but luckily almost all of the people who have supported me in the past are still around for me to thank. Rick Kot may now be a senior editor, but he will always be younger than me. I also hope he will always be my editor. Rick's terrific and helpful assistant, Scott Terranella, has now ascended into the dizzyingly exciting field of publicity. Now, Sheila Gillooly is charmingly and ably doing her best to make my life easier. Debra Elfenbein is a lively and talented production editor; but then again, if I said something negative about her, she'd probably red-pencil the offending item.

Everyone at HarperCollins has been terrific to me, and I would say this even if it didn't score brownie points. Bill Shinker understood the concept of *Imponderables* at the outset and has been enthusiastic and supportive ever since. Brenda Marsh, Zeb Burgess, Pat Jonas, and all the HC sales reps have done a tremendous job; most people who love books don't know how to sell them. These folks do, and with grace and good humor. Steve Magnuson, Robert Jones, and the marketing staff ingeniously strategize about how to foist my books upon an innocent public.

Speaking of foisting upon an innocent public, that is the full-time job of the publicity department. It takes a special person to peddle the tomes of authors with bloated egos to jaded radio and

TV producers. Everyone in the department has been wonderful. Karen Mender leads these special (demented?) types with humor and skill. Thanks to Craig Herman, who is the guy stuck with foisting me.

Connie Levinson, Barbara Rittenhouse, and Mark Landau, of Special Markets, have been, at various times, valuable salespeople, helpers, advisers, psychotherapists, and friends. Thanks for your help. I'm grateful to the entire staff of Special Markets, especially Mary Clifford, for her unsolicited help.

I don't have to be too effusive about my agent, Jim Trupin, since the dedication of this book will probably humor him for a while. Oh, what the heck! He's great. But he'd better continue to treat me well, or I'll complain to his wonderful wife and partner, Elizabeth.

With every book, Kassie Schwan's cartoons get wittier and our collaboration more effortless. I promise to try to provide an Imponderable in every book that will enable you to draw a fish.

Mark Kohut and Susie Russenberger are not only good friends but mentors who have helped me navigate the treacherous waters of publishing.

I've been so busy working this year that I've neglected some friends and family, but they've been there for me. Thanks to all who have lent support: Tony Alessandrini; Michael Barson; Sherry Barson; Rajat Basu; Ruth Basu; Jeff Bayone; Jean Behrend; Brenda Berkman; Cathy Berkman; Sharon Bishop; Carri Blees; Christopher Blees; Jon Blees; everyone at Bowling Green State University's Popular Culture Department; Jerry Braithwaite; Annette Brown; Arvin Brown; Herman Brown; Joann Carney; Janice Carr; Lapt Chan; Mike Chelst; Don Cline; Alvin Cooperman; Marilyn Cooperman; Judith Dahlman; Paul Dahlman; Shelly de Satnick; Charlie Doherty; Laurel Doherty; Joyce Ebert; Pam Elam; Andrew Elliott; Steve Feinberg; Fred Feldman; Gilda Feldman; Michael Feldman; Phil Feldman; Ron Felton; Phyllis Fineman; Kris Fister; Linda Frank; Seth Freeman; Elizabeth Frenchman; Michele Gallery; Chris Geist; Jean Geist; Bonnie Gellas; Richard Gertner; Amy Glass; Bea Gordon;

Dan Gordon; Ken Gordon; Judy Goulding; Chris Graves; Adam Henner; Christal Henner; Lorin Henner; Marilu Henner; Melodie Henner; David Hennes; Paula Hennes; Sheila Hennes; Sophie Hennes; Larry Herold; Carl Hess; Mitchell Hofing; Steve Hofman; Bill Hohauser; Uday Ivatury; Terry Johnson; Sara Jones; Allen Kahn; Mitch Kahn; Joel Kaplan; Dimi Karras; Maria Katinos; Stewart Kellerman; Harvey Kleinman; Mark Kohut; Claire Labine; Randy Ladenheim-Gil; Debbie Leitner; Vicky Levy; Jared Lilienstein; David Lynch; Patti Magee; Jack Mahoney; everyone at the Manhattan Bridge Club; Phil Martin; Chris McCann; Jeff McQuain; Julie Mears; Phil Mears; Carol Miller; Barbara Morrow; Phil Neel; Steve Nellisen; Millie North; Milt North; Charlie Nurse; Debbie Nye; Tom O'Brien; Pat O'Conner; Joanna Parker; Jeannie Perkins; Merrill Perlman; Joan Pirkle; Larry Prussin; Joe Rawley; Rose Reiter; Brian Rose; Lorraine Rose; Paul Rosenbaum; Carol Rostad; Tim Rostad; Susie Russenberger; Leslie Rugg; Tom Rugg; Gary Saunders; Joan Saunders; Mike Saunders; Norm Saunders; Laura Schisgal; Cindy Shaha; Patricia Sheinwold; Kathy Smith; Kurtwood Smith; Susan Sherman Smith; Chris Soule; Kitty Srednicki; Karen Stoddard; Bill Stranger; Kat Stranger; Anne Swanson; Ed Swanson; Mike Szala; Jim Teuscher; Josephine Teuscher; Laura Tolkow; Carol Vellucci; Dan Vellucci; Hattie Washington; Julie Waxman; Ron Weinstock; Roy Welland; Dennis Whelan; Devin Whelan; Heide Whelan; Lara Whelan; Jon White; Ann Whitney; Carol Williams; Maggie Wittenburg; Karen Wooldridge; Maureen Wylie; Charlotte Zdrok; Vladimir Zdrok; and Debbie Zuckerberg.

We contacted about 1,500 corporations, educational institutions, foundations, trade associations, and miscellaneous experts to find the answers to Imponderables that books couldn't answer. We are delighted to say that most sources are becoming more open about sharing information on the record. Although many other people supplied help, all those listed below gave us information that led directly to the solution of the Imponderables in this book. Heartfelt thanks to all: Beth Adams, H. J.

Heinz Company; Dr. Don Adams, Iowa State University; John H. Addington, Fire Equipment Manufacturers Association; John Adinolfi, National Coffee Association; Alamo Rent-A-Car; Stuart Alexander, Deluxe Check Printers; Robert C. Allen, University of South Florida; American Dental Association; Curt Anderson, Sunkist; Jeff Atkinson, Avis.

Rich Barongi, San Diego Zoo; Jaclyn Barrett, *Southern Bride;* J. W. Batchelder; Tara Baugher, West Virginia University; Prof. Donald Beaty, College of San Mateo; Gene Beaudet, *Metalworking News;* Brenda Berkman, New York City Fire Department; Peter Bishop, Ampad; Harold Blake; Jeanette Blum, Public Relations Society of America; Boeing Company; Ray Bombardieri, Southwestern Bell Telephone; Charles A. Bookman, Marine Board; Dr. Albert F. Borges; G. J. Bozant, Fire-End & Croker Corporation; Larry J. Bramlett, National Office Products Association; John D. Brock, Southern Diazo Equipment Company; Ed Bronikowski, National Zoological Park; Richard M. Brooks, Stouffer Hotels; Fred Burgerhoff; Kurt Burghardt, Neodata Services; Dick Burnon, Hertz Corporation; Dr. Kenneth H. Burrell, American Dental Association; Debra Burrell, New York School of Astrology.

Pat Campbell, Bulova Watch Company; Candle Works; Thomas J. Carr, Motor Vehicle Manufacturers Association; Gerry Carr, International Game Fish Association; Bob Carroll, Pro Football Researchers Association; David Cerull, Fire Collectors Club; Joyce Christie, Institute of Public Utilities; Mimi Clark, Pilot Corporation of America; Catherine A. Clay, Florida Department of Citrus; S. Scott Coe, *Sail;* Ernest Collins, United States Postal System; Prof. Richard Colwell, Council for Research in Music Education; Phyl R. Condon, National Football Foundation and Hall of Fame; Mark T. Conroy, National Fire Protective Association; Philip S. Cooke, Inflight Food Service Association; John Corbett, Clairol; Jim Cowen, Roxide International; Richard Cunard, Transportation Research Board.

Dr. Michael D'Asaro; Jim Datka, American Standard; D. Datello, Sharp Electronics; Dr. Frank Davidoff, American College of Physicians; William F. Deal, International Bottled Water Association; Steve Del Priore, Pepsi-Cola Bottling Company of New York; Dr. Dieter Dellman, Iowa State University; Michael DeMent, Hallmark Cards; Nora DiPalma, American Standard; Sara Dornacker, United Airlines; Art Douglas, Lowell Corporation; Leslie D. Downs, Cosmetic, Toiletry and Fragrance Association; Lowell Drutman, Timex Corporation; M. J. Duberstein, NFL Players Association; Thomas Dufficy, National Association of Photographic Manufacturers; Barbara Dwyer, USDA.

Carole L. Edwards, Mobil Oil Corporation; Linda Eggers, Maytag Company; Kay Engelhardt, American Egg Board; Dr. J. Worth Estes, American Association for the History of Medicine; Dr. Howard Evans, Cornell University.

Bill Fabricino, BRK Electronics; Dr. Fred Feldman; Gary Felsinger, Kohler Company; Peter C. Fetterer, Kohler Company; Mike Fisher, Besam Inc.; George Flower; Sam Folsom, Wine Institute; Robert Fontana, TDK Electronics Corporation; James B. Ford; Don French, Radio Shack; Henry Fried.

John A. Gable, Theodore Roosevelt Association; Dr. James Q. Gant, International Lunar Society; Stan S. Garber, Selmer Company; R. Bruce Gebhardt, North American Native Fishes Association; Mark Gerberich, Pro Bowlers Association of America; Glenn Gibson, American Honey Producers Association; Shelly Gilbreath, Southwestern Bell Telephone; Martin Gitten, Consolidated Edison; Anne Glasgow, National Society of Professional Surveyors; Dick Glass, Professional Electronics Technicians Association; William Goffi, *Advertising;* Capt. James E. Grabb, American Society of Naval Engineers; Capt. G. L. Graveson, Naval Submarine League; Barbara Green, Greater New York Hospital Association; Cory Greenspan, Federation of Apparel Manufacturers; Jacqueline Greenwood, Black & Decker; Steve Gregg, Coffee Development Group; Phyllis Grotell, Wool Bureau.

Dr. Robert Habel, Cornell University; Dr. John Hallett, Desert Research Institute, Atmospheric Ice Laboratory; Joseph Hanson, *Folio;* John Harrington, Council for Periodical Distributors; Sylvia Hauser, *Dog World;* David J. Hensing, American Association of State Highway and Transportation Officials; Sanford Hill, American Orthopedic Society for Sports Medicine; Sol Hirsch, National Weather Association; Dick Hofacker, AT&T Bell Laboratories; Jim Hutchison, American Paper Institute.

Embassy of Italy; Barbara Mader Ivey, Women on Wine.

M. Claire Jackson, Coca-Cola; Bill Johnson, California Canning Peach Association; Alvin H. Johnson, American Musicological Society; Robert M. Johnston, Sterling Silversmiths Guild of America; Chris Jones, Pepsi-Cola; Pat Jones, American Association of Port Authorities; Larry Josefowicz, Wilson Sporting Goods Company.

Thomas J. Kallay, Edison Electric Institute; Jeff Kanipe, *Astronomy;* Phil Katz, Beer Institute; Kerry Keller, Center for Christian Studies; William Kemp, Duncan Industries; Debbi Kempton-Smith; Rose Marie Kenny, Hammermill Papers; Hugh Kent, Jr., Internal Revenue Service; Dr. Charles Kesner, Northwest Michigan Horticulture Station; Dr. Ke Chung Kim, Frost Entomological Center, Pennsylvania State University; Dr. Ben Klein; Kevin Knopf, Office of Tax Policy, Department of Treasury; Joan Koenig, Office of Weights and Measures, National Bureau of Standards; Milo Kovar, Astro-Psychology Institute; Thomas P. Krugman, California Cling Peach Advisory Board.

Langenberg Hat Company; John T. Leadmon, Department of the Navy; Dick Levinson, H. Y. Aids Group; Joseph M. Lichtenberg, National Pasta Association; John Loftus, Society of Collision Repair Specialists.

Bridget A. MacConnell, Yuban Coffee; Alan MacRobert, *Sky & Telescope;* Keith Markland, Internal Revenue Service; Serena Marks, United Parcel System; Melanie Martini, *Bride's;* Rudolf H. T. Mattoni, Lepidoptera Research Foundation; James P. McCauley, International Association of Holiday Inns; Karen E. McAliley, United States Postal System; Dr. John R. McCarroll, Methodist Sports Medicine Center; Dennis McClendon, American Planning Association; Frank McDonough, Amerex Corporation; Jody L. Messersmith, Forster Manufacturing; Sally Miller, Procter & Gamble; Dr. Stephen Miller, American Optometric Association; Mr. Coffee; Dr. William E. Monroe, American College of Veterinary Internal Medicine; Sarah Moore, Hills Brothers Coffee, Inc.; Patrick Murphy, *TV Guide*.

John Nasiatka, Duo Fast Corporation; Neckwear Association of America; Embassy of New Zealand; Dr. Richard Nowogrodzki, Cornell University.

Dr. Joe Ogawa, University of California, Davis.

Brad Patterson, Racquetball Manufacturers Association; Neil Patton, Internal Revenue Service; Chuck Pezzano; Robin Pierce, Citizen/CBM America; John A. Pitcher, Hardwood Research Council; Ellen Powley, International Horn Society; Project ELF, Association of Records Managers and Administrators; Roy S. Pung, Photo Marketing Association, International.

Dr. George W. Rambo, National Pest Control Association; Jean C. Raney, American Wool Council; Dr. R. Reed, Redmore Products; Robert M. Reeves, Institute of Shortenings and Edible Oils; Miles Roberts, National Zoological Park; Robot Industries; Dr. Robert R. Rofen, Aquatic Research Institute; Carol Rostad; Prof. Neal Rowell, University of South Alabama; Leslie Rugg; Tom Rugg.

Angela Santoro, *Wall Street Journal;* William Schanen III, *Sailing;* Ronald A. Schuler, California Canning Peach Association; Phyllis Schweers, Thrifty Rent-A-Car System; Norman F. Sharp, Cigar Association of America; Sheaffer Pen; Linda D. Shepler, Sunkist; Rexford B. Sherman, American Association of Port Authorities; Bill Sherrard, Long Island Lighting Co.; Jan Shulman, American Hospital Association; Wayne Smith, Sunbeam Appliance Company; Sid Smith, National Association of Hosiery Manufacturers; Ray Sowers, Tubelite-Indal; Bill Spaniel, Lockheed Aeronautical Systems Company; Margie Spurlock, Royal Crown Cola Company; Dennis W. Staggs, POM Inc.; Bill Stanley; Amy Steiner, American Association of State Highway and Traffic Officials; Dr. Al Stinson, Michigan State University;

John J. Suarez, National Pest Control Association; Amy Sudol, Chase Manhattan; Peggy Sullivan, Music Educators National Conference.

Farook Taufiq, Prince Company; David Taylor, Bank Administration Institute; Dr. Kristin Thelander, University of Iowa; Susan Thompson, A. T. Cross; Susan Tildesley, Headware Institute of America; Randy Troxell, Allied Specialty Company; Catherine Turner, United States Postal System.

Pamela Van Hine, American College of Obstetrics and Gynecology; L. Van Munching, Jr., Heineken; H. T. Vande Kerkhoff, United States Submarine Veterans of World War II; Ralph E. Venk, Photographic Society of America; Roberta Vesley, American Kennel Club.

Dana Walker, Ampad; Mark Weber, Phillips Van Heusen Corporation; Clay Weeks, University of California, Davis; S. C. White, National Hardwood Lumber Association; William O. Whitt, Association of Edison Illuminating Companies; David Williams; Dr. Elizabeth Williams, Wyoming State Veterinary Laboratory; John Williams, California Apple Products Inc.; Richard Williams; Dr. Jack Wilmore, University of Texas; William D. Winter, Jr., Lepidopterists' Society; Eleanor Wulff, International Guild of Candle Artisans.

Wayne Young, Marine Board.

Dr. Richard S. Zack, Washington State University; Dr. E. Zander, Winthrop Consumer Products; and Mike Zazanas, Professional Audio Retailers Association.

And to sources who preferred to remain anonymous, thank you for your help.

WHY DO DOGS HAVE WET NOSES?

Parting Notes

We get the following questions so often in our mail, we thought we'd include our answers to help you understand how *Imponderables* works:

WHY *Didn't You Print My Imponderable in the Last Book?*

Could be a lot of reasons. The biggest mistake most people make is sending in questions that have already been discussed in other books or magazines. If we already know the answer, it isn't an Imponderable anymore. Also, a good Imponderable should be a mystery of *everyday* life, not a theoretical problem, a trivia question, or a query that could be answered by a trip to the dictionary: We're more interested in "why" questions than "who," "what," or "where" questions. And just because you don't see your Imponderable answered in the last book doesn't mean it won't be in the next book.

CAN *I Send in More than One Imponderable at a Time?*

Absolutely. As many as you want. We've received letters with several hundred Imponderables!

DO *You Personally Read Every Letter You Receive?*

Every word.

DO *You Respond Personally to Every Letter?*

Yes, if a self-addressed stamped envelope is enclosed. But depending upon deadline pressures, it might take longer than we'd like. If you don't want or need a personal reply, save the money and send a postcard or a letter without a SASE.

I *Just Bought a Copy of* Why Do Clocks Run Clockwise? *Is It Too Late to Send a Response to the Frustables?*

Probably. We answer the Frustables of one book in the next edition. But if you have something to add to our answers, we always seek corrections and additions. As a rule of thumb, if it is three years or more since the copyright date of the book you are reading, it's too late to send in your answers.

WHAT'S *The Best Time to Send in Imponderables?*

Anytime. We collect Imponderables on a continuing basis. Even if you send in a question after we've stopped researching a current book, we'll save it for the next one.

AFTER *the Name of the Person Who Submitted an Imponderable, It Sometimes Says "Thanks also to" — What Does That Mean?*

It means that the people listed sent in the same or a similar Imponderable after the person who received the "submitted by" credit.

WHO *Is Reponsible for Imponderables That Aren't Credited To Anyone?*

Unattributed Imponderables are usually our ideas, but they also come from anonymous callers on radio talk shows.

WHY *Don't You Group the Imponderables Together by Subject?*

We didn't want to give *Imponderables* the feel of reference books, even if that's the section where they are usually placed in bookstores. We want you to read the book not knowing what to expect next. But if readers feel strongly about this. we'd like to know.

HOW *Can We Make Your Life Easier?*

O.K., we'll admit it. Nobody has ever asked us this question. But may we make one request? Please don't send us money in the mail. We are not equipped to sell books by mail order, and we don't want you to be disappointed if we can't process an order quickly. Most bookstores will special-order books upon request.

Index

Soft drinks, sodium in, 87–88

Sonic booms, 23

Sounds
of burning wood, 10–11
of pay phones, 97–98
of public toilets, 187
after radio is unplugged, 47
sonic booms, 23
telephone rings, 189–90
telephone tones, 129–30
water in pipes, 229

Southern houses, basements in, 98

Soybean oil, 186

Spanish-American War, 49

Sporting events, whistling at, 217

Staples, copper, 90–91

Stars, twinkling, 50–51

State highway numbers, 67

Static electricity, 105–6

Stir frying, 12–13

Stomach, growling, 120–21

Stored product insects, 90

Stouffer Hotel towels, 57

Submarine anchors, 40–41

Subscriptions to magazines, 33–34

Suds, white, from colored soaps, 132

Sugar, in salt, 99

Supersonic aircraft, 23

Swarming of gnats, 3–4

Swatting of flies, 31–32

Table manners, 204–6

Tasmania, 22

Tax form numbers, 9–10

Telephones
busy signals, 182
public, coin sounds, 97–98
sound of ring, 189–90
Special Information Tones, 129–30
twisted cords, 228–29

Television Channel 1, 124

Television set measurements, 37

Temperature
of babies, 103–4
differences in, 184

Temperature *(cont.)*
inversions, 156–57
of water, 151–52
for coffee, 173–74
of wine, 95–97

Terminal dues system (postal rates), 5–6

Thanksgiving, 140–42

Tickle of self, 125

Timepieces, 77–78

Tissue paper in wedding invitations, 116–17

Toes of socks, colored, 19–20

Toilets, public, flushing of, 187

Tongues, stuck out, 215–16

Toothpaste expiration date, 169–70

Toothpicks, mint flavored, 153

Traffic flow, 165–66

Traffic noise, 198

Traps under sinks, 82–83

Triton, orbit of Neptune, 117–18

Tuning pitch for orchestras, 26–27

"Turkey" in bowling, 48–49

TV Guide, 91–92

21-gun salutes, 227

Twinkling of stars, 50–51

Twistoff bottle caps, 145–46

Underwear labels, 4–5

Unimponderables, 122–28

United States highway numbers, 66–67

United States Postal Service
international rates, 5–6
regulations, 149–51
stickers on envelopes, 83–84

University of South Florida, 7–8

UPS trucks, 73–74

Urination of dogs, 35–36

Valve stems on fire hydrants, 142–43

Vegetable oils, 186

Veins, blue, 138

Venice, gondolas, 86–87

Violin bows, frogs of, 164–65

Voices, falsetto, 147–48

Wall Street Journal, 41–42

Washing machine agitators, 56

Watches (timepieces), 77–78, 134–35

Water
bathtub drain, 124–25
for coffee, 173
hot and cold faucets, 191–92
sound in pipes, 229
temperature of, 184
cold, 151–52

Weather patterns, 173–74

Weddings
etiquette, 86
invitations, 116–17

Weigh stations, 193–94

Wetness, and color, 139

Whistling at sporting events, 217

White wine, serving temperature, 96–97

Winds, 156–57

Wine, 95–97

Winter, worms in, 108

Women
menstrual cycles, 100–102
shoes, 229–30
voices of, 147–48

Women's blouses, sleeve length, 113–14

Woodpeckers, 44–45

Wool, wet, smell of, 158–59

Worms
after rain, 109
in winter, 108

Wristwatches, 134–35

Yellow flag in parking meters, 42–43

Yellow pencils, 228

Zodiac signs, dates for, 27–28

INDEX   **249**

Help!

You're probably feeling smug right now. Sure, you've sent in hundreds of great Imponderables for this book.

But what have you done for us lately?

We need more letters.

Letters bursting with Imponderables, answers to Frustables, bouquets, and brickbats. All are welcome and necessary to make future *Imponderables* books as good as they can be.

So join the slightly demented world of Imponderability. If you are the first person to submit an Imponderable we use in the next volume, we'll send you a free copy, along with a fawning acknowledgment in the book.

If you send a self-addressed stamped envelope, we'll reply as quickly as we can, which sometimes, unfortunately, won't be too fast. The SASE is necessary only if you want a reply—all correspondence is welcome.

So send those Imponderables, Frustables answers, and comments, along with your name, address, and (optional) phone number to:

Imponderables
Box 24815
Los Angeles, California 90024